BAPTISTWAY®

Adult Bible Study Guide

Philippians, Colossians, 1 & 2 Thessalonians

Duane Brooks
Ray Pollard
Perry Sanders

BAPTISTWAY PRESS®
Dallas, Texas

Letters to the Philippians, Colossians, and Thessalonians—
Adult Bible Study Guide—Large Print

BAPTISTWAY PRESS® Management Team
Executive Director, Baptist General Convention of Texas: Charles Wade
Coordinator, Church Health and Growth Section: H. Lynn Eckeberger
Director, Bible Study/Discipleship Center: Dennis Parrott

Publishing consultant: Ross West, Positive Difference Communications
Cover and Interior Design and Production: Desktop Miracles, Inc.
Front Cover Photo: The river at Philippi, BiblePlaces.com

First edition: September 2003
ISBN: 1–931060–39–8

How to Make the Best Use of This Issue

Whether you're the teacher or a student—
1. Start early in the week before your class meets.
2. Overview the study. Look at the table of contents, read the study introduction, and read the unit introduction for the lesson you're about to study. Try to see how each lesson relates to the unit and overall study of which it is a part.
3. Use your Bible to read and consider prayerfully the Scripture passages for the lesson. (You'll see that each writer has chosen a favorite translation for each unit in this issue. You're free to use the Bible translation you prefer and compare it with the translation chosen for that unit, of course.)
4. After reading all the Scripture passages in your Bible, then read the writer's comments. The comments are intended to be an aid to your study of the Bible.
5. Read the small articles—"sidebars"—in each lesson. They are intended to provide additional, enrichment information and inspiration and to encourage thought and application.
6. Try to answer for yourself the questions included in each lesson. They're intended to encourage further thought and application, and they can also be used in the class session itself.

If you're the teacher—

A. Do all of the things just mentioned, of course.

B. In the first session of the study, briefly overview the study by identifying with your class the date on which each lesson will be studied. Lead your class to write the date in the table of contents on page 7 and on the first page of each lesson. You might also find it helpful to make and post a chart that indicates the date on which each lesson will be studied. If all of your class has e-mail, send them an e-mail with the dates the lessons will be studied.

C. You may want to get additional adult Bible study comments by Dr. Jim Denison, pastor of Park Cities Baptist Church, Dallas, Texas, that are online at www.baptistwaypress.org and can be downloaded free.

D. You also may want to get the enrichment teaching help that is provided in the *Baptist Standard* and/or on the internet. Call 214–630–4571 to begin your subscription to the *Baptist Standard*. Access the internet information by checking the *Baptist Standard* website at http://www.baptiststandard.com. (Other class participants may find this information helpful, too.)

E. Get a copy of the *Teaching Guide*, which is a companion piece to these lesson comments. It contains additional Bible comments plus two teaching plans. The teaching plans in the

Teaching Guide are intended to provide practical, easy-to-use teaching suggestions that will work in your class.

F. After you've studied the Bible passage, the lesson comments, and other material, use the teaching suggestions in the *Teaching Guide* to help you develop your plan for leading your class in studying each lesson.

G. Enjoy leading your class in discovering the meaning of the Scripture passages and in applying these passages to their lives.

Letters to the Philippians, Colossians, and Thessalonians

1 AND 2 THESSALONIANS
Faith, Love, and Hope

Introducing

PHILIPPIANS: *Rejoicing in Christ*

Think of yourself as writing your life story as you live it, putting the words down by how you live your life. When you start out writing and as you turn each page, are the sheets of paper blank? Not at all, for we are influenced by both our circumstances and our opportunities as we write our story. The story has already been partially written by the various circumstances in which we find ourselves—where we were born, for example, and other aspects of our background. While writing the story of our lives is much more than filling in the blanks, at least a part of our writing this story involves making the best of the circumstances and opportunities we have.

So how can we make the best of life, given the circumstances in which we find ourselves and the opportunities we have? For guidance with such a big question we can turn to a little letter in the New Testament known as Philippians. There we see into Paul's relationship to a small church in Macedonia that he had founded a few years before (see Acts 16:11–40). In the letter we see Paul's warm feelings for the church. Paul called his Christian brothers and sisters in Philippi "my joy and crown" (Philippians 4:1). Paul was grateful for the Philippians and the support they had given him (Phil.1:2–7; 4:10–20). We see Paul's concern, so natural in such a relationship, that his Philippian friends know how things were going with him and of his longing to see them again (1:8, 27). Too, as would be fitting for the Philippian church's founding pastor, Paul wanted the disagreements that the church was experiencing to be healed (2:2–4; 4:2–3). He also wanted the church to live their relationship to Christ in greatest faithfulness (1:27–30). Paul expressed these and other concerns as he wrote.

In and through all of this, the Letter to the Philippians lets us see into Paul's own life as well. Philippians gives us a picture of how Paul was writing the story of *his* life. This letter shows Paul making the best of life, given the circumstances in which he found himself and the opportunities he had.

The immediate circumstance in which Paul was writing was imprisonment (1:12–14). In spite of this, however, Paul's Letter to the Philippians is upbeat rather than somber. A sense of joy, contentment, generosity, and well-being permeates the letter, overflowing from Paul's life.

Traditionally, Paul's Letter to the Philippians has been considered to be set during the time of Paul's imprisonment in Rome. As with many of Paul's letters, pinpointing the exact time and place of writing, however, is not possible with our present knowledge. The Book of Acts, which traces Paul's journeys, does not provide us with verses that state that Paul wrote this or that book in a certain place and at a certain time. So we are left to try to find clues in the letters themselves and attempt to coordinate these clues with what the Book of Acts says. At the same time we are to keep in mind that some of the clues can be interpreted in more than one way and that the Book of Acts does not purport to give us a full biography of Paul. Nevertheless, Paul wrote from some imprisonment, whether Rome (Acts 28:14–31; the late 50s or early 60s, the traditional view), Caesarea (Acts 23:23—26:32; the mid to late 50s), or even Ephesus (for which we have no definite evidence in the New Testament; but see Acts 20:18–19; 2 Corinthians 1:8–10).

Wherever Paul was in prison, we can be sure that the circumstances were not the most pleasant he could have desired and that the opportunities before him were not the widest. Paul, however, made the best of them.

Studying this letter written in the midst of Paul's life situation can help us grapple with our own life situation. As you study this brief letter, watch especially for what it teaches about how you can make the best of the circumstances and opportunities of your life.[1]

PHILIPPIANS: REJOICING IN CHRIST

Additional Resources for Studying Philippians:[2]

Fred B. Craddock. *Philippians*. Interpretation: A Bible Commentary for Teaching and Preaching. Atlanta: John Knox Press, 1985.

Morna D. Hooker. "Philippians." *The New Interpreter's Bible*. Volume XI. Nashville: Abingdon Press, 2000.

Ralph P. Martin. *Philippians*. Revised edition. The Tyndale New Testament Commentaries. Grand Rapids, Michigan: William B. Eerdmans Publishing Company, 1987.

Frank Stagg. "Philippians." *The Broadman Bible Commentary*. Volume 11. Nashville, Tennessee: Broadman Press, 1971.

NOTES

1. Unless otherwise indicated, all Scripture quotations in this introduction and the lessons on Philippians are from the New International Version.
2. Listing a book does not imply full agreement by the writers or BAPTISTWAY PRESS® with all of its comments.

Focal Text

Philippians 1:1–26

Background

Philippians 1:1–26

Main Idea

Although we may need to deal with many negatives in life, we can learn to look at life more positively through practicing our faith in Christ.

Question to Explore

How can we learn to look at life both positively and realistically?

LESSON
ONE

Look at Life Positively

Study Aim

To decide on ways I will approach life positively as well as realistically

Study and Action Emphases

- Affirm the Bible as our authoritative guide for life and ministry
- Share the gospel with all people
- Develop a growing, vibrant faith
- Value all people as created in the image of God
- Equip people for servant leadership

Quick Read

Difficult days usually come to all of us. This lesson can help us understand that we can look at life realistically yet positively because of our faith in Christ.

I can never forget this family. When I called on the family as the new pastor, I found them facing difficulties on every hand. The father had died rather suddenly, leaving his wife in a constant state of near poverty. The only child was handicapped physically and mentally. The mother herself suffered from a debilitating disease of her joints. Yet the home was pervaded by a sense of well-being.

As I left the home, I could not avoid asking how a family could face life in such a positive way when they had so many problems. Our lesson today seeks to give at least a partial answer to this question.

The Book of Philippians shows Paul facing many difficulties. Paul had founded the church at Philippi on his second missionary journey (Acts 16:12–40). When Paul wrote this Letter to the Philippians, he was in prison (Philippians 1:13–14). My view is that the site of his imprisonment was Rome. The Philippians had sent Epaphroditus to look after Paul's needs while in prison. Epaphroditus, however, had become ill, had nearly died, and had been forced to return to Philippi (Phil. 2:25–29). Too, the saints in Philippi, who were so dear to Paul, were facing persecution (1:29). Moreover, their fellowship was threatened by a quarrel between two women (4:2–3). An additional difficulty Paul faced is that there were those who deliberately sought to cause trouble for Paul even while he was imprisoned (1:17).

Yet in all of this, Paul was positive in his outlook. He described his attitude as one of joy (1:4, 18).

Where did Paul find the resources for such a positive outlook given his circumstances? Consider what the Scriptures say.

Philippians 1:1–26

1Paul and Timothy, servants of Christ Jesus,

To all the saints in Christ Jesus at Philippi, together with the overseers and deacons:

2Grace and peace to you from God our Father and the Lord Jesus Christ.

3I thank my God every time I remember you. **4**In all my prayers for all of you, I always pray with joy **5**because of your partnership in the gospel from the first day until now, **6**being confident of this, that he who began a good work in you will carry it on to completion until the day of Christ Jesus.

7It is right for me to feel this way about all of you, since I have you in my heart; for whether I am in chains or defending and confirming the gospel, all of you share in God's grace with me. **8**God can testify how I long for all of you with the affection of Christ Jesus.

9And this is my prayer: that your love may abound more and more in knowledge and depth of insight, **10**so that you may be able to discern what is best and may be pure and blameless until the day of Christ, **11**filled with the fruit of righteousness that comes through Jesus Christ—to the glory and praise of God.

12Now I want you to know, brothers, that what has happened to me has really served to advance the gospel. **13**As a result, it has become clear throughout the whole palace guard and to everyone else that I am in chains for Christ. **14**Because of my chains, most of the brothers in the Lord have been encouraged to speak the word of God more courageously and fearlessly.

15It is true that some preach Christ out of envy and rivalry, but others out of goodwill. **16**The latter do so in love, knowing that I am put here for the defense of the gospel. **17**The former preach Christ out of selfish ambition, not sincerely, supposing that they can stir up trouble for me while I am in chains. **18**But what does it matter? The important thing is that in every way, whether from false motives or true, Christ is preached. And because of this I rejoice.

Yes, and I will continue to rejoice, **19**for I know that through your prayers and the help given by the Spirit of Jesus Christ, what has happened to me will turn out for my deliverance. **20**I eagerly expect and hope that I will in no way be ashamed, but will have sufficient courage so that now as always Christ will be exalted in my body, whether by life or by death. **21**For to me, to live is Christ and to die is gain. **22**If I am to go on living in the body, this will mean fruitful labor for me. Yet what shall I choose? I do not know! **23**I am torn between the two: I desire to depart and be with Christ, which is better by far; **24**but it is more necessary for you that I remain in the body. **25**Convinced of this, I know that I will remain, and I will continue with all of you for your progress and joy in the faith, **26**so that through my being with you again your joy in Christ Jesus will overflow on account of me.

Building Warm Relationships with Others (1:1–8)

Our text makes it clear that Paul had a deep and warm relationship with the Philippians. Note what he said: "I thank my God every time I remember you" (1:3). "In all my prayers for all of you, I always pray with joy" (1:4). "I have you in my heart" (1:7). "I long for all of you" (1:8). In the latter part of 1:8, "with the affection of Christ Jesus," Paul emphasized his feelings by the use of the Greek word *splagchnois*. This word originally meant the internal organs of the human body, such as the heart, lungs, liver, and intestines (thus the KJV translation, "bowels"). It came to mean the seat of the deepest and strongest of feelings of compassion and concern. Note that Paul said he had this feeling for all of the Philippians.

Both the cause and effect of such strong emotions can be found if we look at the relationship Paul had experienced with the Philippians. Philippians 1:5 says it was because of their "partnership." This word translates the Greek word, *koinonia*, which we all too often understand simply as *fellowship*,

> . . . I could not avoid asking how a family could face life in such a positive way when they had so many problems.

meaning to share a social event. The word means much more. It means to share in labor and sorrow as well as to share in having a pleasant time together.

That they so shared can be seen if we remember the Philippians had sent Epaphroditus to meet Paul's needs (2:25). They had also supported Paul's ministry when others had not (4:14–15). Paul encouraged this warm relationship by praying for them, thanking God for them, rejoicing because of them, and commending them for their fellowship in the gospel (1:3–7).

Paul's warm relationship with the Philippians in his time of difficulty should remind us that others can play a great part in helping us get through bitter times. They can not only help us to survive but also to thrive in such times.

> *Paul's warm relationship with the Philippians in his time of difficulty should remind us that others can play a great part in helping us get through bitter times.*

Relating to Others with Concern (1:9–11)

Ironically, one of the best helps we have in getting through difficult times is to focus not on self but on others and their needs. Paul made it clear that he cared for the saints in Philippi. Now he demonstrated that concern by his prayer for them. Note the content, the character, and the consummation that he sought in his prayer for them.

In his prayer Paul sought two things: love and knowledge. He did not specify any item or person he sought for the Philippians to love. Rather his intent seems to have been that love would be a guiding principle in their life. This of course would mean loving others and loving God. The love that he prayed for them to have was a love known by its giving of self for the well-being of others. Love is active and not merely an emotional state. The word translated "love" in 1:9, *agape*, is a form of the same word used of God's love for a lost world as found in John 3:16. The knowledge Paul sought for them was more than intellectual information. It was a knowledge that made clear what was best for them.

Ironically, one of the best helps we have in getting through difficult times is to focus not on self but on others and their needs.

What Paul was seeking was that they might be pure in motive and activity and that they might be blameless until "the day of Christ" (1:10), referring to Christ's second coming. Furthermore he was concerned that they not only avoid doing the wrong things but rather that they also do the right things. This is what is meant by " . . . filled with the fruit of righteousness" (1:11).

If the Philippians experienced these things and so lived as to make them a part of their life, God himself would be glorified and praised. Shouldn't this be the goal of our lives as Christians?

The happiest people in the world are not necessarily those with no obvious pain in their lives. Neither are the most contented people those who are constantly seeking self-gratification. Rather the happiest people in the world are those people who in spite of their own difficulties reach out and seek the best for others.

Looking for the Good Even in the Midst of Opposition (1:12–19)

Paul had opponents who were against him personally and against the spread of his gospel. He was in chains because of his preaching. The extended story of Paul's arrest that led to his imprisonment in Rome is found in Acts 21—26. Some Christians were opposed to Paul for unspecified reasons. Yet Paul's arrest gave the opportunity to share the gospel even with the palace guard (1:12–13). Furthermore, even these Christian opponents of Paul were preaching the gospel (1:15). In addition, some of Paul's more timid fellow Christians had been

. . . The happiest people in the world are those people who in spite of their own difficulties reach out and seek the best for others.

encouraged to be more courageous in their testimony (1:14). The result was that the gospel was spread. It was spread in ways that would have never been possible without the difficulties Paul faced.

Difficulties are often opportunities for growth and progress. What at first seems to be bad news can in fact be good news.

Recently I spoke to a man who said that the best thing that had ever happened to him was being so seriously injured that he had to change professions. Out of that forced redirection of his life, he had opened his own business. Now he had a much greater income, a more stable family life, and greater opportunity to do the things he enjoyed.

. . . The focus of Paul's life was on Christ. . . . Here was the secret of Paul's positive outlook even in the worst of circumstances.

This is the meaning, in part, of what Paul said in Romans 8:28: "And we know that in all things God works for the good of those who love him, who have been called according to his purpose." Note that Paul did not say that all things that happened were good. Rather he said that God was working for good in the midst of them.

Focusing Life on Christ (1:20–26)

We have already noted that Paul was having a difficult time. The church in Philippi, which was so dear to him, was divided. Some of Paul's fellow Christians were acting out of envy and rivalry (1:15). Some were deliberately seeking to cause him trouble (1:17). Furthermore, Paul was in prison (1:13). Even more, he apparently knew he might be facing a death sentence, for he spoke clearly of his potential death (1:21–23).

Yet in these circumstances, Paul continued to rejoice (1:19). How could he rejoice in such circumstances? The answer is to be found in the focus of his life. Paul's life was not focused or built around personal comfort or worldly achievements. Rather the focus of Paul's life was on Christ. He was quite clear about this, saying, "For to me, to live is Christ and to die is gain" (1:21). Here was the secret of Paul's positive outlook even in the worst of circumstances. This same option is ours if we so choose.

Difficulties are often opportunities for growth and progress.

We can do many things to keep our life focused on Christ. We can make a priority in our daily schedule of having a regular time of prayer and devotion. We can actively participate in our church. We can consciously reach out to others in need. We can examine as honestly as we can our motivation for living as we do. We can seek to bring glory to Christ. We can remember the promises and provisions God has given us as God's children.

What About Us?

Recall the family mentioned at the first of this lesson. They had many serious problems. Yet they maintained a positive outlook. The question was raised as to how this could be. How could they remain so upbeat when others with lesser problems give in to despondency and despair? We find our answer in the experience of Paul as reflected in Philippians 1.

Using Paul as our example, we find that he maintained a positive outlook by building warm relationships with others, by relating to others with concern, by looking for the good even in the midst of opposition, and by focusing his life on Christ. With these guidelines, we can look at life realistically and yet retain a positive outlook.

Overseers, Elders, and Deacons

The New Testament uses three words to describe two offices in churches. The word translated "overseer" (Philippians 1:1; Titus 1:7) and the word translated "elder" (Titus 1:5) refer to the same office.

Some Christian groups today draw a distinction between the two words but without biblical support. An "overseer" was one who served as a superintendent or guardian. The "elder" was so titled because of age and responsibility.

Then there is the word translated "deacon" (Phil. 1:1). In the secular world of New Testament times, this word was used commonly and was applied to one who served.

Case Study

John Doe is an active member of your church. Recently his adult but unmarried son came home to die of AIDS. Since then John has expressed many negative feelings. He feels he has been deserted by his church family since he is no longer invited to visit and others no longer visit his home. How should his church respond to him and his family?

Questions

1. How does faith in Christ aid one in facing the painful days of our lives?

2. If you were asked to bring a devotional on facing life's difficulties, what would you say in the devotional?

3. What has been your greatest comfort during difficult times?

4. What is the single greatest Christian truth that helps us through troublesome times?

Focal Text

Philippians
1:27—2:15

Background

Philippians
1:27—2:18

Main Idea

Living a life worthy of the
gospel calls for following Christ in
a life of humility, concern for
serving others, and faithfulness,
whatever the cost.

Question to Explore

Are you living a life worthy
of the gospel?

LESSON TWO

Live a Life Worthy of the Gospel

Study Aim

To describe what it would mean to make the Jesus Paul pictured truly my Lord

Study and Action Emphases

- Affirm the Bible as our authoritative guide for life and ministry
- Share the gospel with all people
- Develop a growing, vibrant faith
- Obey and serve Jesus by meeting physical, spiritual, and emotional needs
- Equip people for servant leadership

Quick Read

The purpose of this lesson is to understand what it would mean to make the Jesus Paul pictured Lord. Included in doing so would be humility, concern for serving others, and faithfulness whatever the cost.

This person gave every evidence of being a true and devout disciple of Christ. His moral standards and behavior could not be questioned. His prayer and devotional life were exemplary. He was as good a personal friend and supporter as a pastor could ever hope to have. He was as faithful and devoted a deacon as a church ever had.

All of this is why I was so appalled and surprised when he told me he was unworthy and was withdrawing from many church activities. When I questioned him as to why this was so, he replied that there was friction over some financial affairs between himself and another church member. Furthermore, he said he felt a great deal of bitterness, hostility, and anger toward the other individual. That being so, he stated that he was unworthy to be a deacon or leader in the church.

Let's examine this person's statements. Was he unworthy? What qualities make a person worthy or unworthy? That is the question we would explore in today's lesson. Our text makes several suggestions.

Before we look at Paul's advice as to what it means to live a life worthy of the gospel, let us look at his reasons for it. You will remember that the church at Philippi was divided. This is why Paul appealed to them to "stand firm in one spirit, contending as one man for the faith of the gospel" (Philippians 1:27). A specific example of this is the feud between Euodia and Syntyche that Paul mentioned (Phil. 4:2). This division evidently had led to complaining and arguing, or at least Paul was concerned that it might (2:15). Too, as Paul ministered, even in prison, he faced opposition by people who were motivated by envy and rivalry and not love and humility (1:15).

None of this reflected the character of Christ, who should have been the example these Christians sought to imitate (2:5). Christ's whole attitude was one of humble service. This attitude of Christ was utterly contrary to that of the prevailing norms of their society. Their society promulgated the idea that service to others was the demeaning place of a slave. Furthermore, their society believed that public praise and recognition, not service, should be a major goal of life. In this writer's opinion, things have not changed all that much from their day to ours.

Let us now look at the suggestions Paul made to combat these problems that were hindering the work of the gospel. He instructed the saints in Philippi to ". . . conduct yourselves in a manner worthy of the gospel of Christ" (1:27). Our text gives three suggestions of things to do to live a worthy life. Such a life calls for having a courageous unity in the face of opposition, having the mind of Christ, and making our Christian life complete.

Philippians 1:27–30

27Whatever happens, conduct yourselves in a manner worthy of the gospel of Christ. Then, whether I come and see you or only hear about you in my absence, I will know that you stand firm in one spirit, contending as one man for the faith of the gospel **28**without being frightened in any way by those who oppose you. This is a sign to them that they will be destroyed, but that you will be saved—and that by God. **29**For it has been granted to you on behalf of Christ not only to believe on him, but also to suffer for him, **30**since you are going through the same struggle you saw I had, and now hear that I still have.

Philippians 2:1–15

1If you have any encouragement from being united with Christ, if any comfort from his love, if any fellowship with the Spirit, if any tenderness and compassion, **2**then make my joy complete by being like-minded, having the same love, being one in spirit and purpose. **3**Do nothing out of selfish ambition or vain conceit, but in humility consider others better than yourselves. **4**Each of you should look not only to your own interests, but also to the interests of others.

5Your attitude should be the same as that of Christ Jesus:

6 Who, being in very nature God,
   did not consider equality with God something to
      be grasped,
7 but made himself nothing,
   taking the very nature of a servant,

being made in human likeness.
8 And being found in appearance as a man,
he humbled himself
and became obedient to death—
even death on a cross!
9 Therefore God exalted him to the highest place
and gave him the name that is above every
name,
10 that at the name of Jesus every knee should bow,
in heaven and on earth and under the earth,
11 and every tongue confess that Jesus Christ is Lord,
to the glory of God the Father.

12Therefore, my dear friends, as you have always obeyed—not only in my presence, but now much more in my absence—continue to work out your salvation with fear and trembling, **13**for it is God who works in you to will and to act according to his good purpose.

14Do everything without complaining or arguing, **15**so that you may become blameless and pure, children of God without fault in a crooked and depraved generation, in which you shine like stars in the universe. . . .

Being Worthy Requires a Courageous Unity in the Face of Opposition (1:27–30)

The church in Philippi was a small group of Christians in the midst of a much larger population. The church was having troubles. Some of the troubles were internal. The members obviously were not unified

(1:27). Too, they were frightened by their opposition (1:28). They were facing persecution. Recall that when Paul and Silas had established the church in Philippi, they had been beaten and thrown into prison because of their Christian activities (Acts 16:16–24).

All of this is why I was so appalled and surprised when he told me he was unworthy and was withdrawing from many church activities.

Philippians 1:29 has an interesting thought. There Paul said the Philippian Christians had been granted the privilege of suffering for Christ. The word he used for "granted" is the Greek word for grace. That is to say their suffering for Christ was a gift of love. Did you ever consider suffering for Christ as an act of God's love and grace?

Paul appealed to the Philippians to " . . . conduct yourselves in a manner worthy of the gospel of Christ" (Phil. 1:27). As noted earlier, this worthy lifestyle includes at least three elements. We now look at the second element.

Being Worthy Means Having the Mind of Christ (2:1–11)

As we examine this passage of Scripture, we need ever to remember this one important truth: Jesus is God in the flesh. However we explain this passage of Scripture, and it can be difficult to explain it, our explanation cannot be in conflict with this great truth.

Our passage falls into two parts. The first part (2:1–4) describes how the Philippians should live. The second part (2:5–11) points to Christ as an example they should imitate. Both parts grow out of the appeal for the Philippians to "conduct yourselves in a manner worthy of the gospel of Christ" (1:27).

A careful reading of 2:2 will make clear that Paul's great concern for the Philippians was that of unity. He appealed to them on the basis of their being united with Christ, of sharing Christ's love, of being compassionate, and of making Paul's joy complete by being united. He then pointed out the causes of disunity. Disunity came from living egocentric lives governed by selfish ambition, vain conceit, and pride. He appealed to the Philippian Christians to live instead a life governed by being concerned for others, as did Jesus.

Such a life calls for having a courageous unity in the face of opposition, having the mind of Christ, and making our Christian life complete.

The second part of our passage deals with the person of Christ and with the example Christ gives to his people to imitate. Paul said it succinctly when he stated, "Your attitude should be the same as that of Christ Jesus" (2:5). Who is Jesus and what was and is his attitude?

In describing the nature of Christ, Paul used two words very deliberately. The word "being" in 2:6 refers to unchanging essence. The thought is that the very nature of Christ was that of God. In 2:7 Christ is described as taking the "nature" or appearance of a slave. Jesus did not cling to his deity but rather took the form of a slave for the benefit of humankind. This act demanded even his crucifixion as an act of obedience. Such an act calls for the world to confess that Jesus is truly Lord of all (2:10–11).

Being Worthy Means Making Our Discipleship Complete (2:12–15)

Here we have a Pauline paradox. Paul made it quite clear that salvation is from God. But in the same breath, Paul appealed to the Philippian saints to work out their own salvation. That salvation is the gift of God and not something we earn is emphasized in many ways in Scripture. Paul's whole argument in Romans 3—4 is that Abraham was saved by the grace of God and not by any works on Abraham's part. Note how concisely and clearly Paul stated this great truth in such places as Ephesians 2:8–9. Philippians 2:13 restates this truth when it says, "For it is God who works in you to will and to act according to his good purpose."

Did you ever consider suffering for Christ as an act of God's love and grace?

While salvation is the work of God, the people of God are called on to "work out" their salvation

36

(Phil. 2:12). The word translated "work out" (2:12) means to bring to completion. People are called on to complete the work God seeks to do in them. In other words, to live a worthy life is not one of passive quietism. We are saved by grace, but it is a part of our discipleship that "we are God's workmanship, created in Christ Jesus to do good works, which God prepared in advance for us to do" (Ephesians 2:10).

This effort is to be done "with fear and trembling" (Phil. 2:12). This fear is not the cringing fear of slaves wondering whether their master will beat them or make them suffer in some worse way. Rather it is a fear that so great a love as God has will be hurt as his servants seek to bring their salvation to completion.

> *Whatever else these verses mean, they mean that all that is done must be done without complaining and bickering.*

Whatever else these verses mean, they mean that all that is done must be done without complaining and bickering. The final goal of such efforts will be that saints will become blameless and pure and without fault in a corrupt world.

What About Us?

In Philippians 1:27 Paul used a word filled with meaning. Remember that the people of Philippi lived as Roman citizens and that they were proud of their citizenship. They spoke Latin, dressed as Romans, and lived under Roman law. Paul used a word that means to live as a citizen (translated "conduct yourselves").

To a Roman, being a Roman citizen meant at least two things. It meant privilege. When Paul was arrested and about to be scourged, he asked whether it were legal to treat a Roman citizen so (Acts 22:22–29; see also 16:37). Learning Paul was a citizen, the Roman commander was frightened that he had come so close to violating Roman law by punishing a Roman citizen without a trial. Being unjustly hauled before Festus, Paul appealed to Caesar (Acts 25:11).

We have the responsibility of living in a way worthy of the God who loves us and the world to such an extent that God became a man and died that we might live and share the gospel with others.

Being a Roman citizen also meant responsibility. Paul's arrest in Philippi created a major uproar when the accusation was made that he advocated living contrary to Roman law (Acts 16:20–23).

To be a Christian has these two aspects. First, we have many privileges. We have the privilege of having been given forgiveness—that is, having our sins and faults not present a barrier between God and us. Too, we have faith, something to believe in a world filled with uncertainty. Also, we have a family, fellow believers with whom we should share a fellowship. In addition, we have a future, something to look forward to.

Second, we also have a responsibility. We have the responsibility of living in a way worthy of the God who loves us and the world to such an extent that God became a man and died that we might live and share the gospel with others.

Who Is Jesus?

One of the greatest internal conflicts Christianity has ever faced occurred in the fourth century AD and was about the relationship of Christ and God the Father. A Christian leader named Arius said that Christ had a nature and was of a substance *similar* to God. Those who opposed Arius said that Christ had a nature and was of the *same* substance as God.

Simply stated, Arius and his followers said Jesus was not divine but was a created being. This is the position of Jehovah's Witnesses today. It was condemned, however, in 325 AD at the Council of Nicea, which rejected the view of Arius and declared that Christ was in fact God and a human being at the same time. We cannot fully comprehend or explain this truth, but it remains our faith.

Envy

Envy nearly wrecked the early missionary efforts of Baptists here in America. Today we are firmly committed to missions, but this commitment came only after an intense struggle. Briefly this is what happened. In 1812 Adoniram Judson and Luther Rice sailed for Burma as Congregationalist missionaries. While at sea they studied the Greek New Testament and became convinced that Baptists were more biblical in their positions. They believed this was especially true of baptism.

In order to gain financial support and promote missions in general, Rice returned to America. At first he was quite successful. In 1814 he led in the formation of the Triennial Convention, whose major purpose was missions. Associations and churches committed themselves to the support of missions.

In a few years, however, many of these same associations and churches reversed themselves. A major reason was envy. Many of the preachers from frontier America were unlearned and uneducated. They envied and opposed the educated leaders who supported missions.

Case Study

She was angry and vehement in her denunciations of me as pastor and of the church as a whole. She had phoned my office, and as soon as I answered, she began her tirade. It took me several minutes to get her calmed down enough to understand why she was angry. She was angry, and she finally said so clearly, because neither she nor her family was being given the recognition and accolades to which they were entitled for their various contributions to the church. How should I have responded to her?

Questions

1. What is the major source of envy in an individual?

2. How can envy best be defeated in the life of a Christian?

3. What should be done about Christians whose life is obviously not worthy of the gospel they profess to hold?

4. Why is it important to understand that Jesus is truly God incarnate?

Focal Text

Philippians
2:19–30

Background

Philippians
2:19–30

Main Idea

People who make a difference for
Christ give of themselves in
serving others for Christ's sake.

Question to Explore

What kind of people should we be
honoring?

**LESSON
THREE**

Make a Difference with Your Life

Study Aim

To determine to become a person who makes a difference for Christ

Study and Action Emphases

- Affirm the Bible as our authoritative guide for life and ministry
- Share the gospel with all people
- Develop a growing, vibrant faith
- Include all God's family in decision-making and service
- Value all people as created in the image of God
- Obey and serve Jesus by meeting physical, spiritual, and emotional needs
- Equip people for servant leadership

Quick Read

Great accomplishments of any kind require strong commitments. This is certainly true of Christianity. People who accomplish things for Christ give of themselves in serving others.

If we are to become people who make a difference for Christ, then everything we do is involved. Our daily life and routine activities are as much a part of our service as are our distinctly religious activities. That is why we should not be surprised to see Paul make an abrupt transition from that great hymn-like passage on the nature and work of Christ that we studied in the previous lesson and begin talking about the day-to-day lives of Timothy and Epaphroditus.

The transition between 2:18 and 2:19 seems almost jarring at first glance. The transition is such that some scholars have suggested that Paul intended to end Philippians at this point. If, however, we stop and think for a moment, we shall find the transition not nearly as abrupt as first appears. What we see in this lesson is how these two servants of Christ and companions of Paul lived out the "attitude" that was "the same as that of Christ Jesus" (Philippians 2:5).

Philippians 2:19–30

19I hope in the Lord Jesus to send Timothy to you soon, that I also may be cheered when I receive news about you. **20**I have no one else like him, who takes a genuine interest in your welfare. **21**For everyone looks out for his own interests, not those of Jesus Christ. **22**But you know that Timothy has proved himself, because as a son with his father he has served with me in the work of the gospel. **23**I hope, therefore, to send him as soon as I see how things go with me. **24**And I am confident in the Lord that I myself will come soon.

25But I think it is necessary to send back to you Epaphroditus, my brother, fellow worker and fellow soldier, who is also your messenger, whom you sent to take care of my needs. **26**For he longs for all of you and is distressed because you heard he was ill. **27**Indeed he was ill, and almost died. But God had mercy on him, and not on him only but also on me, to spare me sorrow upon sorrow. **28**Therefore I am all the more eager to send him, so that when you see him again you may be glad and I may have less anxiety. **29**Welcome him in the Lord with great joy, and honor men like him, **30**because he almost died for the work of Christ, risking his life to make up for the help you could not give me.

Timothy: Serving Without Wavering (2:19–24)

Timothy was a native of Lystra, which was located in what is now the south central part of Turkey (Acts 16:1–2). Legally he was a Jew since his mother was Jewish, even though his father was a Gentile. Any child born to a Jewish mother was considered to be Jewish, although a child with a Jewish father was not necessarily considered to be so. The name of Timothy's mother was Eunice (2 Timothy 1:5). Apparently his mother did not practice her faith, because Timothy was not circumcised as an infant (Acts 16:3).

We do not know how Timothy became a Christ-ian, although it is often assumed he came under the influence of Paul on Paul's first missionary journey (Acts 14:8–23). When Timothy is first mentioned, he already had a good reputation as a Christian. Paul chose him to accompany Silas and himself as they continued the second missionary journey (Acts 16:3). Timothy served Paul many years as a close associate. Paul called him "our brother" (1 Thessalonians 3:2), "God's fellow worker," (1 Thess. 3:2), and "my son whom I love, who is faithful" (1 Corinthians 4:17).

If we are to become people who make a difference for Christ, then everything we do is involved.

At times in the company of Paul and at times without Paul being present, Timothy worked to spread the gospel and strengthen the work. The work of Timothy was not always easy. In Philippi there was conflict (Acts 16:16–40). When Paul sent Timothy back to Corinth to deal with the many problems of the church, Timothy evidently was not able to correct the problems, although he helped to establish the work (1 Cor. 4:17; 16:10; 2 Cor 1:19). Note how Paul felt it necessary to appeal to the church to receive Timothy, saying, " . . . see to it that he has nothing to fear while he is with you. . . . No one, then should refuse to accept him. Send him on his way in peace" (1 Cor. 16:10–11).

There are at least two outstanding things about Timothy and his work. One was that he worked so faithfully and so long in good days and in bad. The other was that he was always subservient to Paul. Much of Timothy's work was serving as Paul's emissary. Paul sent Timothy to serve as his emissary on a number of occasions.

In our text Paul sent Timothy to Philippi to learn how things were there and to carry a message from Paul. He sent Timothy to Thessalonica "to strengthen and encourage you in your faith" (1 Thess. 3:2). He sent him to Corinth to deal with the many problems of that church (1 Cor. 4:17).

Look at some of the biblical materials for these two truths for a moment. Paul said that he had no one like Timothy and described why Timothy was such a faithful worker (Phil. 2:19–22). In the first place, Timothy took a genuine interest in the welfare of the Philippians (2:20). The word "genuine" originally referred to a son born in wedlock and not out of wedlock. It came to mean that which is true and not spurious. Second, Timothy did not look after "his own interests" (2:20). Contrast this to what Paul said about the motives of some others in 1:15–18. Finally, Timothy was truly concerned about the things of Christ (2:21).

Some disciples, even though occupying prominent places, can have wrong motives.

Things have not changed. Some disciples, even though occupying prominent places, can have wrong motives. Take for example an educational director I knew. In terms of knowing how church organizations

47

and programs should be organized, planning training opportunities to equip church workers, and knowing how to evaluate a church budget, he was the best I ever knew. In some ways he was the best educational director his church had ever known. He never, however, seemed to be happy or satisfied. One day I asked him why. He replied, "It bothers me to know that I will never be the leading member of a church staff. It bothers me that the pastor will always have that position and not me. It irritates me that I will never get the recognition that comes so easily to him."

When he left my office that day, I felt humbled and unworthy to serve as pastor to such as him.

Epaphroditus: Serving at Great Cost (2:25–30)

As we look at Epaphroditus in our text, let us remember that this is not the Epaphras associated with the church at Colossae. Epaphras is a shortened form of Epaphroditus, and both were fairly common names when the New Testament was written. Men given this name were often from families who worshipped Aphrodite. Aphrodite was the ancient goddess of sex and love. All that we know of Epaphroditus, not Epaphras, is in Paul's Letter to the Philippians (2:25–30; 4:18). He is not mentioned any place else in the New Testament.

Epaphroditus was an outstanding member of the church in Philippi. When Paul wrote Philippians, he was in prison. The church had sent Epaphroditus to meet the needs of Paul. This entailed meeting Paul's financial needs and meeting other unspecified needs (4:18). While with Paul, Epaphroditus became so sick that he nearly died. With Paul's commendation, he returned to Philippi. Paul told the church to "welcome him in the Lord with great joy, and honor men like him" (2:29). It was true that Epaphroditus was homesick (2:26). Paul made sure, though, that the Philippian church did not view Epaphroditus as one who out of his homesickness or other reasons failed to carry out his assigned task.

Notice how this emissary from Philippi to Paul is described. Paul specifically called him three things. He is "brother, fellow worker, and fellow soldier" (2:25). As a brother, Epaphroditus shared a spiritual kinship with Paul. As a fellow worker, he shared in the missionary activity of Paul. As a soldier, he shared in the dangers faced by Paul as together they faced enemies of the gospel. Paul said, "He almost died for the work of Christ" (2:30). Paul also called him the "messsenger" from the church at Philippi (2:25). The word translated "messenger" is actually the Greek word for *apostle*, although here it does not mean one of the twelve apostles of Jesus. It simply means one sent as a representative.

To make a difference for Christ is within the reach of every disciple.

Years ago I had a church member who reminded me of this early disciple. When I first went to the church as a young pastor, Hugh came to see me. Today he would be described as one of the "working poor." He obviously had limited financial means. His language was that of one with a very limited education. When he left my office that day, I felt humbled and unworthy to serve as pastor to such as him. What he said with words and attitude were the words of a servant of Christ. He assured me that even though he had no money and no education, he did have something to give to his Lord. He could give his skill as a "fixit man" and his sweat in manual labor. In the days to come I found this to be true. If a faucet dripped, a casual mention of it to Hugh resulted in a quick repair. If plumbing became clogged, he cleared it. If a hinge squeaked, he lubricated it. He summed up his discipleship one day when he said, "I ain't got no money, but I can see to it that God's people got no need to apologize for where they worship." As age and sickness took its toll on his life, he continued his service day after day. The last time I saw him before his death, he apologized for not being physically able to do a needed minor repair job at the church.

Some of the most valuable people are those performing mundane and menial tasks.

Faithful service, not envious ambition, should be our motive.

What About Us?

To make a difference for Christ is within the reach of every disciple. In the very nature of things, there will be some who are far more visible than others and who hold more prominent positions within the body of believers. This does not mean that they are more valuable to the kingdom of God. Some of the most valuable people are those performing mundane and menial tasks. The important thing is not how much recognition we receive. Neither is specifically what we do important. Rather it is our motivation in faithfully doing the things that are our responsibility. Faithful service, not envious ambition, should be our motive.

What bothers me is how many church members are not willing to overly exert themselves in their chosen ministry and service.

Having served as a pastor for near fifty years, something has always bothered me. What bothers me is how many church members are not willing to overly exert themselves in their chosen ministry and service.

Let me give you an example that I shall always remember. Doing as I have often done, I preached one time quoting my text and speaking without notes. After the service, a young man approached me and said, "Preacher, God has called me to preach and I have surrendered my life to preaching. But how did you recite your text from memory and preach without notes?"

As I described hours of work and sweat in preparation, he began to look discouraged. Finally he said as he turned and walked away, "I done knowed they was a catch to it."

Servant, Minister

The NIV, in this writer's opinion, erred when it failed to translate specifically one word in Philippians 2:25 (compare translations; see especially NASB and NRSV). The Greek word is *leitourgos*. It has several meanings. As a religious word it meant to serve as a priest or priestly helper. As a government word, it meant to serve as a government official. As a civic word it meant to render some great service to one's community. This is the word Paul used to describe Epaphroditus when Paul said of him, "whom you sent to take care of my needs" (2:25).

Walter Rauschenbusch

Walter Rauschenbusch (1861–1918) was probably the most influential and most controversial Baptist preacher and professor of his day. He served as pastor of the Second German Baptist Church in an area of New York City known as Hell's Kitchen. There he saw the effects of poverty, discrimination, alcohol, and unrestrained capitalism and greed. Furthermore, he saw the results of government indifference.

Driven in part by a vision of the Old Testament denunciation of the oppression of the weak and helpless, he denounced these social evils in the strongest possible terms. While he did not originate the term, he was the most visible exponent of a social gospel, which held that the Christian church should seek to redeem lives as well as souls.

Questions

1. To what extent does sharing the gospel involve such things as schools, child care facilities, feeding hungry people, etc.? Can we engage in "full gospel" activities and completely ignore such things?

2. Paul is certainly the best known and probably the most influential follower Jesus ever had. Timothy and Epaphroditus are less known. How important is it to be well-known and even influential?

3. Can you name some ways in which all of us can not only share how to be saved but can also meet other human needs?

4. How can we involve the shy and timid in sharing the gospel? What tasks can such folks assume that will make use of their talents and skills?

5. How important are the disciples who do not give great gifts financially or stand before a group and teach but whose service is found in such ways as Hugh served?

Main Idea

Living life the best way consists of valuing Christ supremely and engaging in the lifelong quest to know Christ fully.

Question to Explore

If you reached your goal in life, where would you be?

LESSON
FOUR

Keep Focused on Knowing Christ

Study Aim

To commit or recommit myself to valuing Christ supremely and seeking to know Christ fully

Study and Action Emphases

- Affirm the Bible as our authoritative guide for life and ministry
- Share the gospel with all people
- Develop a growing, vibrant faith
- Value all people as created in the image of God

Quick Read

Knowing Christ and continuing to grow in knowing him is of supreme importance in life. Salvation includes not just being converted but also continuing to walk with Christ and pressing on toward the culmination of salvation, which is yet to come.

As Christians we are sometimes guilty of a serious mistake. We emphasize the necessity of an individual's turning to Christ in repentance and faith. We earnestly invite people to turn to Christ for the forgiveness of their sin. This is as it should be. The error is we find it so easy to stop here. We, by act if not by theology, limit the meaning of salvation to this saving experience. However, the Bible, which is our authority under Christ, teaches that the initial experience is only the beginning of salvation. It teaches that to be a Christian is a lifelong quest to know Christ fully. Our purpose today is to understand at least in part what this means and to commit our life to making it our goal in life. We do this not simply because we believe the Bible teaches it but because this is the way to have the best possible life.

Philippians 3:2–14

2Watch out for those dogs, those men who do evil, those mutilators of the flesh. **3**For it is we who are the circumcision, we who worship by the Spirit of God, who glory in Christ Jesus, and who put no confidence in the flesh—**4**though I myself have reasons for such confidence.

If anyone else thinks he has reasons to put confidence in the flesh, I have more: **5**circumcised on the eighth day, of the people of Israel, of the tribe of Benjamin, a Hebrew of Hebrews; in regard to the law, a

Pharisee; **6**as for zeal, persecuting the church; as for legalistic righteousness, faultless.

7But whatever was to my profit I now consider loss for the sake of Christ. **8**What is more, I consider everything a loss compared to the surpassing greatness of knowing Christ Jesus my Lord, for whose sake I have lost all things. I consider them rubbish, that I may gain Christ **9**and be found in him, not having a righteousness of my own that comes from the law, but that which is through faith in Christ—the righteousness that comes from God and is by faith. **10**I want to know Christ and the power of his resurrection and the fellowship of sharing in his sufferings, becoming like him in his death, **11**and so, somehow, to attain to the resurrection from the dead.

12Not that I have already obtained all this, or have already been made perfect, but I press on to take hold of that for which Christ Jesus took hold of me. **13**Brothers, I do not consider myself yet to have taken hold of it. But one thing I do: Forgetting what is behind and straining toward what is ahead, **14**I press on toward the goal to win the prize for which God has called me heavenward in Christ Jesus.

A Misplaced Confidence (3:2–6)

Prior to his conversion, Paul depended on his heritage to make him righteous in the sight of God. He warned the Philippians against making his mistake by placing their confidence in the wrong things.

Apparently there was in Philippi a recognizable group who taught that the way to worship God demanded circumcision. Three times in the Greek of verse 2 Paul used the definite article "the" as he described those whom he called dogs, who did evil, and who were "mutilators of the flesh." These are strong terms. Paul was so vehement because of what was at stake. This group's attitude was very narrow and sectarian. It said that unless you were "one of them," you were automatically wrong. Underlying these words is the unspoken question, "What must I do to be saved?" In the strongest of terms, Paul said that circumcision of the flesh is not the answer. Making a play on words that is lost in our English translation, he wrote that "we" are the true circumcision and his opponents are mere mutilators of the body.

When questioned about her hope for eternity, she would point to her childhood experience and almost flippantly say she had been saved and could never be lost.

To make his point even stronger, Paul pointed to his own heritage. His parents were not simply descendants of Abraham. They were also of the tribe of Benjamin. Furthermore, they observed the law by having Paul circumcised according to the law. Finally, as an adult, Paul was a Pharisee and as such strictly observed the things his opponents said were the requirements for a right relationship. He summed up his position by saying he was faultless in his observance of the law but that this was nothing in comparison to knowing Christ.

The point of this discussion of a misplaced confidence is simply that legalistic observances and rituals are not sufficient to gain a right standing with God. Neither can an individual depend on the faith of his or her family to suffice.

Note also that Paul was pointing out that a narrow sectarian spirit divided God's people instead of uniting them in a common fellowship. The church at Philippi is not the only church to have experienced such sectarianism—and misplaced confidence. Such attitudes and behaviors are still alive and well. Let me briefly illustrate what I mean.

Some people depend on the life of loved ones to suffice for them. Paul's parents reared him according to the tenets of the law, but Paul said such a heritage was insufficient. Having parents who are devoutly religious is insufficient for their children. Having devout parents is desirable, but it is not enough. Legalistically doing religious things likewise is insufficient for a right standing with God. Attending church, tithing, serving on committees—such activities are all good, but they do not earn us God's favor. Finally, to demand that all agree with every minute choice of mine simply creates barriers between people who are brothers and sisters in Christ.

Paul did not want merely to know about Christ; rather, he wanted to know Christ.

A Complete Salvation (3:7–11)

Paul described salvation as a righteousness to be found by faith in Christ. This salvation is more than being guiltless before the law. Rather it has an impact on all of life. Note how Paul portrayed his life in Christ.

First, Paul had a new sense of values. The things that he once considered to be his profit are considered to be instead "loss" (3:7) and "rubbish" (3:8). Paul declared nothing is as valuable as knowing Christ. It is not simply that Paul's heritage was of less value to him than knowing Christ. Rather, anything this world had to offer was of less value. Paul called the things of the world "rubbish" (3:8). The word "rubbish" is used to describe such things as scraps of food left over from a meal and unfit to eat. It even refers to human sewage. All things short of knowing Christ are seen to be as such. All of these things now counted for nothing.

Paul warned against believing that we have become perfect.

Second, Paul had a new goal in life. His new values grew out of his new goal in life. This goal was to know Christ and to become like Christ. Paul did not want merely to know *about* Christ; rather, he wanted to *know Christ*. Let me explain. I knew a man whose hobby was learning all he could about General George Patton of World War II fame. The man could tell you Patton's date of birth and death. He could tell you Patton's height, weight, and color of hair and eyes. He knew the brand of cigarettes Patton smoked and the books Patton read. He had, however, never met Patton. He knew about him, but he did not know him. Such information is not the kind of knowledge Paul desired to have of Christ. He wanted to experience Christ in daily life, to know and to obey Christ's will. In so doing, Paul wanted to become like Christ.

. . . Paul's past accomplishments would not suffice for the present, and neither would past failures destroy today's opportunities.

Third, Paul had a new understanding of how to achieve righteousness, referring to a right relationship with God. Before, Paul sought such a relationship by the observance of external rites, rituals, and regulations. As a Pharisee he was meticulous in keeping the myriad regulations that were seen to be a part of God's will for people. Paul now knew that a right relationship with God came from faith in Christ.

Fourth, Paul had a new hope of sharing in the final resurrection. Although he did not explicitly say so, clearly he had in mind the resurrection where God will claim his own. Note carefully that Paul did not casually assume that he would share in that resurrection. It was his fervent wish to do so.

Paul's attitude, at this point, was far from that of Peggy. Peggy responded to an evangelistic appeal in her church when she was a child. She was baptized and for some years was quite active in the affairs of her church. When she reached adulthood and was married, she lost all interest in Christianity. She never attended church, never prayed (except in emergencies!), never read her Bible. When questioned about her hope for eternity, she would point to her childhood experience and almost flippantly say she had been saved and could never be lost. Paul, however, never took his final salvation for granted.

A Needed Warning (3:12–14)

Paul warned against believing that we have become perfect. Perfection is our goal, but it is always beyond our grasp. In making this point, Paul stated several truths quite clearly.

In the first place, Paul had not fully attained his goals and certainly did not consider himself to be perfect. Although he had given years of his life to attain his goals and though he was now in prison for his efforts, there was yet more to be accomplished.

Perfection is our goal, but it is always beyond our grasp.

In the second place, Paul's past accomplishments would not suffice for the present, and neither would past failures destroy today's opportunities. Paul forgot the past in his struggle to go forward.

Then, too, Paul still struggled to achieve perfection. Such perfection was always just beyond his grasp.

Finally, Paul struggled to achieve his ultimate goal of knowing and being like Christ. This was the prize for which he struggled to make his own.

Sam Snead at one time was considered to be the best golfer in the world. An incident from his life explains at least partially how he reached such a height. Snead had just won a major tournament. The next morning some newspaper reporters wanted to interview him. They found him practicing. He told them he

. . . Paul had not fully attained his goals and certainly did not consider himself to be perfect.

should have done better and hoped to do so next time. That was Paul's attitude toward his Christian experience.

What About Us?

Our background text closes with Paul describing the Philippians as "my brothers," "my joy and crown," and "dear friends" (4:1). Clearly Paul valued them and their relationship. It was to such people whom he had appealed to stand firm in the Lord knowing what it meant to daily seek to " . . . know Christ and the power of his resurrection" (3:10). Such an appeal comes to us, too, even though we may consider ourselves "good Christians." Let us hear and respond.

The Pharisees

Our text is the only place in the New Testament where Paul identified himself as a Pharisee. Who were the Pharisees? The question is important because of the role they played in the life of Christ and of Paul. The name itself probably comes from a root word meaning *separate*. Their historical roots go back to the Jewish Exile in the sixth century BC. During that time, when the Jewish people were deprived of the temple and its elaborate priestly rituals, they sought to retain their cultural and religious identity. Although not generally priests, the Pharisees were noted for their strict adherence to the Mosaic law as they understood it. This meant a commitment to tithing, Sabbath observance, and other ancient rituals. As a political and religious sect, the Pharisees sought to make Israel conform to their view of what it meant to be the chosen people of God.

Case Study

Peter belongs to a church that teaches that after an individual is truly converted by repentance and faith in Christ, there remains another work of God's grace in the person's heart. The church's belief is that when certain conditions are met, the Holy Spirit will "sanctify them holy" or give them "the second blessing." This second work of God's grace, according to Peter's church, renders it possible for an individual to live a life that is nearly perfect and is in fact sinless.

Peter, in speaking to a friend, said that he had received this second blessing and was in fact so holy that he could not even be tempted to sin. In light of Jesus' command, "Be perfect, therefore, even as your heavenly Father is perfect" (Matthew 5:48), and in light of Paul's testimony (Phil.3:12) and admonition (3:15), how do you respond to Peter's claim?

Circumcision

In Philippians 3:5, Paul referred to his circumcision. What is the meaning and significance of circumcision? The origins and original meanings of circumcision are lost in history. It was practiced by many peoples around the Mediterranean Sea. Today as it was for centuries before the birth of Paul, it is observed by Jewish people on the eighth day of an infant's birth. It has, however, in other cultures been practiced at the onset of puberty, at the time of marriage, and at the time of becoming a part of the Hebrew covenant people of God.

Circumcision has great significance to the Jewish people. It testifies to participating in the covenant God made with them. Its practice was repugnant to the Greeks, however. Jewish people were sometimes forced to choose between being faithful to the teachings and traditions of their people or being accepted in the society in which they lived.

In Christ

Paul often used the phrase "in Christ" in his writings. What does it mean? Sometimes it comes very close to meaning simply that someone is a Christian. It means that Christ is the instrument by which we receive the blessings of God's grace. Being "in Christ" is not a once-for-all experience of coming to know Christ as Savior and Lord. This is true no matter how moving and meaningful such an experience might be. Rather it speaks of a daily communion with Christ in every aspect of our life. This thought can perhaps be illustrated by what was said of the young man who had just given his fiancé an engagement ring. It was said of him, "He is so wrapped up in that girl that he cannot think of anything else."

Questions

1. What are some unworthy goals in life? What are some worthy goals in life?

2. Why is valuing Christ supremely and engaging in the lifelong quest to know Christ fully the best goal in life?

3. What are some of the greatest hindrances to knowing Christ more fully?

4. What are some of the best ways to experience Christ and the power of Christ's resurrection?

5. What can a local church do to encourage its members to engage in the lifelong quest to know Christ and to experience the power of Christ's resurrection?

Main Idea

A life of genuine joy and contentment comes not from our external situation but from putting our faith in the Lord into practice.

Question to Explore

What brings genuine joy?

LESSON FIVE

Live with Genuine Joy

Study Aim

To decide to put into practice at least one action from which true joy in life comes

Study and Action Emphases

- Affirm the Bible as our authoritative guide for life and ministry
- Share the gospel with all people
- Develop a growing, vibrant faith
- Obey and serve Jesus by meeting physical, spiritual, and emotional needs
- Equip people for servant leadership

Quick Read

Christians should have joy in their lives. Real joy does not come from external circumstances but rather from practicing the virtues of our faith.

Consider Paul's situation when he wrote the inspiring words of this lesson's Scripture passage. He was in prison chained to a Roman guard. He was facing a probable death sentence. Some of his dearest friends and supporters in Philippi were fighting among themselves. Furthermore, they were being threatened by the society in which they lived.

Under these circumstances, Paul wrote a letter from prison to his friends in Philippi. The letter has as a central thought the joy he had. He said that he is always offering prayer "with joy" (Philippians 1:4). He wrote, "I will continue to rejoice" (Phil. 1:18). He said, "But even if I am being poured out like a drink offering . . . I am glad and rejoice . . ." (2:17–18). In the four short chapters of Philippians, Paul used the words *joy* or *rejoice* more than a dozen times.

What is true joy? Is joy the passing pleasure of a pleasant evening with friends? Is joy to be found in having an easy life with creature comforts? Our purpose is to explore such questions.

As we explore these questions, we will find that real joy is more than a pleasant evening with friends. Furthermore, it is not to be found in having creature comforts. As we explore, we will find that genuine, abiding joy in life comes from practicing the virtues in our Christian faith.

The circumstances of life that create tensions and troubles of various kinds should not be denied. Still, they should neither prevent nor destroy the joy of a Christian. But how can that be? As we study this lesson, let us consider four suggestions about having joy that come from the experience of Paul.

Philippians 4:2–19

2I plead with Euodia and I plead with Syntyche to agree with each other in the Lord. **3**Yes, and I ask you, loyal yokefellow, help these women who have contended at my side in the cause of the gospel, along with Clement and the rest of my fellow workers, whose names are in the book of life.

4Rejoice in the Lord always. I will say it again. Rejoice! **5**Let your gentleness be evident to all. The Lord is near. **6**Do not be anxious about anything, but in everything, by prayer and petition, with thanksgiving, present your requests to God. **7**And the peace of God, which transcends all understanding, will guard your hearts and your minds in Christ Jesus.

8Finally, brothers, whatever is true, whatever is noble, whatever is right, whatever is pure, whatever is lovely, whatever is admirable—if anything is excellent or praiseworthy—think about such things. **9**Whatever you have learned or received or heard from me, or seen in me—put it into practice. And the God of peace will be with you.

10I rejoice greatly in the Lord that at last you have renewed your concern for me. Indeed, you have been concerned, but you had no opportunity to show it. **11**I am not saying this because I am in need, for I have learned to be content whatever the circumstances. **12**I know what it is to be in need, and I know what it is to have plenty. I have learned the secret of being content in any and every situation, whether well fed or hungry, whether living in plenty or in want. **13**I can do everything through him who gives me strength.

14Yet it was good of you to share in my troubles. **15**Moreover, as you Philippians know, in the early days of your acquaintance with the gospel, when I set out from Macedonia, not one church shared with me in the matter of giving and receiving, except you only; **16**for even when I was in Thessalonica, you sent me aid again and again when I was in need. **17**Not that I am looking for a gift, but I am looking for what may be credited to your account. **18**I have received full payment and even more; I am amply supplied, now that I have received from Epaphroditus the gifts you sent. They are a fragrant offering, an acceptable sacrifice, pleasing to God. **19**And my God will meet all your needs according to his glorious riches in Christ Jesus.

Live with Genuine Joy by Remembering (4:2–5)

As we look at these verses, several items call for our attention. The first is that our text is quite clear that Christians should "rejoice . . . always" (4:4). We are not directed to rejoice only when all is well. We are commanded by our text to "rejoice . . . always." But note that this rejoicing is "in the Lord" (4:4). That is, our rejoicing is to be found in our abiding fellowship with the Lord and our dependence on the Lord's power and grace.

Second, we are called on to let our "gentleness be evident to all" those about us (4:5). The word "gentleness" is broadly defined. It means such things as *patience* and *good will*.

Then, we are reminded that "the Lord is near" (4:5). The emphasis here likely is not the expectation that Christ would shortly return to this earth. Paul's future travel plans and his potential death seem to eliminate this interpretation. Rather, the phrase is a reminder that Christians always live in the presence of God.

The Philippians were having a difficult time. A serious division between two women threatened the unity of the church (4:2). Too, false teachers were confusing believers (3:2). If this were not enough, the Philippian Christians were facing persecution by the unbelieving society in which they lived

What is true joy?

(1:29). Under these circumstances, Paul called on the Philippians to respond with patience and good will to all concerned, remembering that they lived in the very presence of Christ.

It is against this background that Paul gave the instructions to "rejoice . . . always" (4:4). Clearly the joy of which Paul spoke is not simply a light-hearted gaiety. It is rather an abiding peace and contentment, knowing that our lives are in the hand of a loving

73

God. Such a conviction rules out a mean-spirited desire for revenge on those who might oppose us.

Live with Genuine Joy by Praying (4:6–7)

Verse 6 entreats the Philippians to do two things. One is not to be anxious—not to fret, worry, or be frightened—about anything. The second is to pray. In Paul's appeal for prayer, he used two separate words. One means essentially to worship God or to come into God's presence. The word speaks of an attitude. The other word is more narrow and means to make a request. Prayer should be done with an attitude of thanksgiving.

. . . Genuine, abiding joy in life comes from practicing the virtues in our Christian faith.

The promised result is that we will have a peace that comes from God that is greater than our mind can comprehend. In addition to this, we are promised that this peace will "guard" our hearts and minds (4:7). "Hearts" speaks of our emotion, and "minds" of our intellect. The promise is that if we have the peace of God that comes from prayer, this peace will prevent our being emotionally and intellectually distraught.

Not to be anxious does not mean not to care. We should care deeply about some things. What not being anxious means is that we ought not to be afraid. To live in emotional turmoil brought on by anxiety is to doubt the goodness and ability of God to provide for our needs.

A humorous yet serious example of worry occurred in my ministry many years ago. A person called and made a counseling appointment. She began the discussion by describing how worried and frightened she was. She had difficulty in sleeping, suffered from an upset stomach, and had other symptoms that she attributed to worry. When she finished describing how her worry affected her physically and emotionally and spiritually, I asked the simple question of why she was so worried. Her reply was at first quite confusing. She said she was worried because she had no reason to be worried. She then went on to describe the problems that her friends and neighbors had and

> *. . . Rejoicing is to be found in our abiding fellowship with the Lord and our dependence on the Lord's power and grace.*

the disasters that had come into their lives. She finished by telling how great her life was. Her husband adored her and provided a good living for the family. Her children were the kind to make a parent proud. She concluded by saying the reason she was so worried was because she knew that when something went wrong, it would be terrible. She was afraid that God would "even the score" by giving her troubles to match her blessings. Verse 7 reminds us, however, of how we can count on God.

Live with Genuine Joy by Thinking About the Best Things (4:8)

In verse 8, Paul gave a list of eight virtues. These were not distinctly Christian virtues. They were well-known to the Stoics of his day. Let's look at these for a moment.

The Christian should think on things that are "true." Some things make promises they cannot keep and are at best deceptive. We should focus our thoughts on what is true.

> ... Our lives are in the hand of a loving God.

The Christian should think on things that are "noble." This is a difficult and complicated word to translate. Comparing various translations will illustrate the point. The basic thought is that a Christian should think on things worthy of God.

The Christian should think on things that are "right." The word translated "right" is from the same root word that means *just*. It means to meet the requirements of the rules.

Another virtue is purity. This virtue carries the idea of being morally cleansed. When used in religious rituals, it means appropriate and dedicated to God.

"Lovely" is the next virtue. It means that which is appealing and that which calls forth the best in another.

"Admirable" is another word difficult to translate. It carries the idea of that which has a good name or that which is fit to hear.

Still another virtue is that which is "excellent." It means the very best of its kind whether speaking of a tool, an animal, or anything else. The Christian should think only of the best things.

To live in emotional turmoil brought on by anxiety is to doubt the goodness and ability of God to provide for our needs.

"Praiseworthy" is the final virtue. The Christian should not live for the praise of others. However, the Christian should think about the things that elicit praise from others.

Nature abhors a vacuum. This idea is true in the physical world, and it is true with our minds. Our minds will be filled with something. Some thoughts are unworthy of a Christian. The appeal is that we fill our minds with meditation on these virtues. There is a reason for this. We become what we think.

Live with Genuine Joy by Imitating Paul (4:9–19)

Paul closed this letter by calling on the Philippians to imitate him (4:9). He wrote that they should practice whatever they had heard or observed in him. His emphasis was that their knowledge and their actions should be in harmony with each other. After this appeal, he mentioned at least four practices or attitudes.

First, Paul called attention to the fact that he had learned to be content and satisfied in all circumstances

(4:10–12). Against this background, he said, "I can do everything through him who gives me strength" (4:13). The thought is that God will give the ability to endure and remain true to God's calling. The meaning is not that we can work miracles of a thousand different kinds.

Second, Paul expressed thanksgiving for the help the Philippians had given him (4:14). You will remember that they had sent Epaphroditus to aid him and Epaphroditus had brought some financial help (2:25; 4:18). Paul's expression of thanksgiving reveals at least two important matters. One is that Paul was truly thankful (4:14–16). Another is that the Philippians' giving was as much for their benefit as it was for his (4:17).

Many devout Christians with great faith have known what it means to be terribly sick and to live in poverty.

Perhaps the testimony from a few years ago from one of the members of the church I serve will reinforce this point. Our church was running behind in its budget. Finances were tight. We put on a stewardship campaign that was aimed at far more than increasing the size of our offerings. Its purpose was to teach our people the meaning of giving self in service to others and the cause of Christ. When the emphasis was ended, a faithful member commented that no one knew the blessings he had received because of the knowledge that he had a vital part in meeting human needs and in supporting evangelism and missions.

Consider for a moment Philippians 4:19. In this writer's opinion, this verse has been terribly misconstrued in the minds of some. This verse is not a promise that God will grant us perfect health and personal wealth. Many devout Christians with great faith have known what it means to be terribly sick and to live in poverty. Their condition is not automatically to be attributed to a lack of faith on their part. A "name-it-and-claim-it" theology is simply wrong.

> *God will give the ability to endure and remain true to God's calling.*

What About Us?

If there is any joy in this world, Christians should have it. After all, we have a Lord who loves us more than our minds can comprehend. This Lord not only offers forgiveness and reconciliation by faith but also offers strength for daily living and a promise of a better tomorrow.

Case Study

Ms. Jones and Ms. Smith were both in the hospital at the same time and by sheer chance were in the same room. Both had chronic debilitating health problems. Both were widows and lived alone. Each had one son who was happily married and lived in a distant state. There the many similarities ended.

Ms. Jones was miserable and unhappy. She complained bitterly about her son. She said he called only once a week. He never came home except at Christmas and while on his summer vacation. She called him an ungrateful wretch who ought to give up his job and move back into her home.

Ms. Smith on the other hand had a smile that brightened the day. She spoke of her son's love and concern and the fact he never let a week go by without phoning her. He never missed coming home at least twice a year. She spoke of his professional success and his happy marriage. She said emphatically that she was blessed in more ways than she could count.

These two women in such similar circumstances raise an interesting question. How can we account for one's misery and the other's joy?

Questions

1. It is hard to be joyful when we are having great difficulties. Why is this so? Is it lack of faith or a preoccupation with the wrong things? Is it something else?

2. It is clear that Christians should have a great measure of joy in their life. How successful is the typical Christian at this?

3. Stoicism taught that the complete person did not need friends or loved ones. Having such was a matter of indifference. What do you think of this idea, especially in light of Philippians 4:11–13?

4. Our text gives a list of eight virtues (4:8). If you could change this list by adding one or more virtues, what virtues would you add? Which two or three of these virtues do you consider most important?

5. Our text lists several aids to having a deep and abiding joy. What one item do you think is the greatest help to having joy?

Introducing

COLOSSIANS: *Christ over All*

Who or what takes priority in life? In this letter to the church at Colosse, the answer to that question is made unmistakably clear. Christ is to take priority in life. "He is before all things, and in him all things hold together" (Colossians 1:17).[1]

Exactly why the Colossian Christians needed to be reminded of the important truth that Christ is over all and that there should be no rival to Christ, in either ideas or practices, is not clear. Various suggestions have been given about the nature of what is sometimes called the "Colossian heresy." Perhaps some in the church had been affected by some of the religious and philosophical ideas that swirled about in the first-century world and that would have been found in the Greco-Roman culture of Colosse. Perhaps the challenge came from the Jews in Colosse. They may have insisted that keeping the Jewish laws and rituals was important and had thus drawn some Christians into—or back into—such practices. Perhaps what was misleading the Colossian Christians was a mixture of these influences.

Colosse was located in the Roman province of Asia. This ancient area was in the western portion of what we know as modern-day Turkey. Although we don't know for sure whether Paul ever went there, we have pretty strong evidence that his influence reached there even prior to this letter. When Paul preached in Ephesus for two years, "all the residents of Asia, both Jews and Greeks, heard the word of the Lord" (Acts 19:10). "All the residents of Asia" would have included the Colossians. Too, in addition to Paul's contacts with Ephesus and likely also with Colosse, Paul also had close contacts with the neighboring town of Laodicea, only ten miles away. Laodicea is referred to in Colossians 2:1 and 4:13, 15–16. So Paul knew the Colossians well and cared deeply for them (Col. 1:3–4; 2:1).

The Letter to the Colossians may have come near the middle of Paul's missionary ministry or it may have come toward the end. If Paul wrote Colossians toward the end of his ministry, the time would have been in the early 60s during his imprisonment in Rome.

Whatever the exact nature of the problem the Colossian Christians faced, the Letter to the Colossians gave pointed instructions about how to deal with it. We will see the main lines of these instructions in the lessons to be studied. The letter called on the Colossian Christians to put Christ first rather than to follow competing ideas. The letter also called these first-century Christians to stop trying to find life in keeping rituals and rules. The letter further challenged them to focus on their life in Christ and live up to their Christian commitment in their daily living. Look back at the previous three sentences, which capsule the three lessons to be studied in Colossians. Any chance we might need the same instructions?

COLOSSIANS: CHRIST OVER ALL

Additional Resources for Studying Colossians:[2]

James D.G. Dunn. *The Epistles to the Colossians and to Philemon*. The New International Greek Testament Commentary. Grand Rapids, Michigan: William B. Eerdmans Publishing Co., 1996.

Andrew T. Lincoln. "Colossians." *The New Interpreter's Bible*. Volume XI. Nashville: Abingdon Press, 2000.

R.E.O. White. "Colossians." *The Broadman Bible Commentary*. Volume 11. Nashville, Tennessee: Broadman Press, 1971.

NOTES

1. Unless otherwise indicated, all Scripture quotations in this introduction and the lessons on Colossians are from the New International Version.
2. Listing a book does not imply full agreement by the writers or BAPTISTWAY PRESS® with all of its comments.

Main Idea

Because Christ is supreme in revealing God and providing reconciliation, Christ deserves the supreme place in our lives.

Question to Explore

Who or what is number one in your life?

LESSON SIX

Who's Number One?

Study Aim

To identify who Christ is and decide how I will put Christ in first place in my life

Study and Action Emphases

- Affirm the Bible as our authoritative guide for life and ministry
- Share the gospel with all people
- Develop a growing, vibrant faith
- Obey and serve Jesus by meeting physical, spiritual, and emotional needs
- Equip people for servant leadership

Quick Read

Jesus Christ's exclusive work in the creation and redemption of the world uniquely qualifies him to claim primacy over all things. When we recognize Christ's love manifested in creation and the crucifixion, we receive Christ's supremacy over our own lives.

Who is really number one? During the fall of the year, football players and teams across the country assert their claims to supremacy on the gridiron.

Other athletes demand attention by their personalities. Boxing champion Muhammad Ali claimed, for example, to be "the greatest." A story alleges that Ali was on an airplane and refused to wear a seatbelt. The flight attendant attempted several times to win his compliance, all to no avail. Finally, she pleaded one more time with him. He defiantly insisted, "I'm superman. Superman doesn't need a seatbelt."

She prevailed by answering, "Superman doesn't need an airplane. Put on your seat belt!"

If we as human beings are not the greatest, then who is? Paul answered that question for us in Colossians 1:1–23.

Colossians 1:1–23

1Paul, an apostle of Christ Jesus by the will of God, and Timothy our brother,

2To the holy and faithful brothers in Christ at Colosse:

Grace and peace to you from God our Father.

3We always thank God, the Father of our Lord Jesus Christ, when we pray for you, **4**because we have heard of your faith in Christ Jesus and of the love you have for all the saints—**5**the faith and love that spring from the hope that is stored up for you in heaven and that you have already heard about in the word of truth, the gospel **6**that has come to you. All over the world this gospel is bearing fruit and growing, just as it has been doing among you since the day you heard it and understood God's grace in all its truth. **7**You learned it from Epaphras, our dear fellow servant, who is a faithful minister of Christ on our behalf, **8**and who also told us of your love in the Spirit.

9For this reason, since the day we heard about you, we have not stopped praying for you and asking God to fill you with the knowledge of his will through all spiritual wisdom and understanding. **10**And we pray this in order that you may live a life worthy of the Lord and may please him in every way: bearing fruit in every good work, growing in the knowledge of God, **11**being strengthened with all power according to his glorious might so that you may have great endurance and patience, and joyfully **12**giving thanks to the Father, who has qualified you to share in the inheritance of the saints in the kingdom of light. **13**For he has rescued us from the dominion of darkness and brought us into the kingdom of the Son he loves, **14**in whom we have redemption, the forgiveness of sins.

15He is the image of the invisible God, the firstborn over all creation. **16**For by him all things were created: things in heaven and on earth, visible and invisible, whether thrones or powers or rulers or authorities; all things were created by him and for him. **17**He is before all things, and in him all things hold together. **18**And he is the head of the body, the church; he is the beginning and the firstborn from among the dead, so that in everything he might have the supremacy. **19**For God was pleased to have all his fullness dwell in him, **20**and through him to reconcile to himself all things, whether things on earth or things in heaven, by making peace through his blood, shed on the cross.

21Once you were alienated from God and were enemies in your minds because of your evil behavior. **22**But now he has reconciled you by Christ's physical body through death to present you holy in his sight, without blemish and free from accusation—**23**if you continue in your faith, established and firm, not moved from the hope held out in the gospel. This is the gospel that you heard and that has been proclaimed to every creature under heaven, and of which I, Paul, have become a servant.

Supreme in Reconciling Us to Himself (1:1–14, 19–23)

Paul began the Letter to the Colossians by telling the Colossian Christians how he thanked God for them because of their "faith in Christ Jesus" and "the love you have for all the saints" (Colossians 1:4). This faith and love were based on "the hope that is stored up for you in heaven" (Col. 1:5). Paul also told of how the gospel itself was "bearing fruit and growing," not just among the Colossians but all over the world. Paul then wrote of his continuing desire that the Colossians might "live a life worthy of the Lord and . . . please him in every way" (1:10). He then enumerated some actions included in pleasing God in "every way": "bearing fruit in every good work, growing in the knowledge of God, being strengthened with all power . . . and joyfully giving thanks to the Father" (1:10–12).

The Colossian congregation evidently was a great church, worthy of Paul's praise and prayers. They, though, were not "the greatest." Paul quickly moved to talk about the One who truly is "the Greatest."

Paul described how, through the crucifixion, Jesus had "rescued us from the dominion of darkness and brought us into the kingdom of the Son he loves, in whom we have redemption, the forgiveness of sins" (1:13–14). In these verses we see that Jesus has rescued us, received us into his kingdom, and redeemed us from our sins. Consider what Jesus did for the Colossians and for us.

Who is really number one?

First, Jesus rescued us and delivered us from the death of darkness and the darkness of death. Do you recognize your helplessness to save yourself from sin?

When we could not save ourselves, God through Christ came and delivered us. He then transferred us from "the dominion of darkness" into the kingdom of the Son," bringing "redemption, the forgiveness of sins" to us (1:13–14). Jesus purchased us, "making peace through his blood, shed on the cross" (1:20).

In Romans 5:6–10, Paul told another group of believers that while we were alienated from God, Christ came and died for us. We were enemies of God. Then God reconciled us to himself through Christ. Furthermore, God is not reconciled to us, but we are reconciled to him. God doesn't ultimately come around and see it our way, but God does invite us to see it his way.

In Colossians 1:20–23 we discover that while we were alienated from God, he reconciled us to himself through Christ's death and made us pure before God. This means we could not get better on our own. It took God's mercy and grace.

We see Jesus' fingerprints on the created world.

People often speak these days about how they found God. The reality, though, is that we didn't find God; God found us. We are likewise in error when we boast about how we have made our peace with God. Upon what basis did we make peace with God? God made peace with us through the blood of God's own Son!

Supreme over All Things (1:15–17)

In creation, Jesus asserted his supremacy over all things. The Maker reserves the right to do with his creation whatever he will. We see Jesus' fingerprints on the created world. Every molecule testifies to his creative power.

As the introduction to the Letter to the Colossians in this *Study Guide* suggests, the exact nature of the erroneous religious views the Colossian church was having to confront is uncertain. One element of the problem, though, could have been the beginnings of the religious philosophy known as Gnosticism (see article, "Gnosticism"). Gnosticism would have placed Jesus as one in a long line of emanations from God. Against such a view, Paul clarified that Jesus is "the image of the invisible God,"

> *To a bargain-hunting culture, the story of the gospel is the greatest deal of all.*

meaning the exact representation of God's being (1:15). We also see this teaching in John 1:1–18 and Hebrews 1:1–4.

In addition, Jesus is "the firstborn over all creation" (1:15). The idea is not that Jesus was the first creation of God but rather that Jesus was of first importance in the act of creation. He was the *logos* or Word who was with God from the beginning and was God from time immemorial (see John 1:1–3).

Why does it matter whether God created us? The answer is that if there is no Designer of the created order, then we owe no allegiance and no accountability to the purpose of the Creator. To deny God's work in creation becomes an excuse for disobeying God's teachings.

The story is told of a person challenging God to a man-making contest. Proudly he said to God, *I can make a better human being than you can.* God accepted his challenge under the condition that they follow his original procedures. When it came time to begin, the man gathered a handful of dirt. God said, *Wait a minute. You have to get your own dirt!*

Christ's supremacy over all things extends to us. In his praise to Christ's work in creation, Paul pointed out that "all things were created by him and for him" (1:16). That includes us. Christ created us by his power for his purpose. What was God's great purpose in creation? He wanted fellowship, communion, and intimacy with humankind.

> *Only God can fill the God-shaped vacuum or void in our lives.*

The church father Augustine put that thought like this: "You have made us for yourself, and our hearts are restless until we rest in you."[1] Is that why we are so restless? Have we not found rest in God? Only God can fill the God-shaped vacuum or void in our lives.

We know that Jesus *created*. Jesus still *creates*! Paul wrote in 2 Corinthians 5:17 (NRSV), "If anyone is in Christ, there is a new creation: everything old has passed away; see, everything has become new!"

Supreme over the Church (1:18)

Who is in charge of your church? After Paul thanked God for the Colossians' faith, hope, and love, he reminded them of Christ's supremacy over the church. Indeed, as the hymn text affirms, "The church's one foundation is Jesus Christ her Lord; she is his new creation, By Spirit and the Word"![2]

The crescendo comes in Colossians 1:18, "That in everything, he might have the supremacy." Isn't that your prayer for your church—that Christ would become renowned as the leader of his church and that every knee would bow and every tongue would confess the universal supremacy of Christ?

Upon what basis can Jesus claim to be the head of the church? Paul twice used the word "firstborn" to say that Jesus was first in creation and in the resurrection (1:15, 18). The word "firstborn" does not focus on time but on importance. Christ stands supreme over all other authority. Not only does Jesus stand first in the universe as the agent of creation, but Jesus also asserted his supremacy in the resurrection. Even though others in the Bible had died and been brought back to life from death, they died again. Only Jesus arose and remains alive eternally. In these two acts—Jesus' creation of the world and Jesus' resurrection from the dead—Jesus proved once and for all that he alone is the Lord of the universe and the church.

In view of all that Christ has done, can any of us ever accurately say, This church is mine?

Our assistant pastor Michael Reynolds, his wife Katherine, their daughter Lauren, and I were at a restaurant along with Josh Guajardo, the pastor who supervises all of our mission churches. Michael was trying to teach his daughter about the church. Michael asked her, "Who is the Senior Pastor?" Pointing to Josh and then to me, Michael pressed, "Who is the boss of the church?" A perceptive little girl, precocious Lauren looked at Josh and me as one might look at a police lineup or the pictures on the wall in the post office. Then she rolled her eyes as if to say, *Daddy, I don't know who it is, but it isn't one of these guys.* She was right.

Either Christ is first, or we are first! Which is it?

If we are wondering who is in charge of the church—the pastoral staff, the deacons, the committees—the answer is, *None of the above!* None of us created the church, and none of us died on a cross for the church. We all, though, have been rescued, redeemed, and reconciled through Jesus by whom all things were created and who is also the crucified and risen Lord.

In view of all that Christ has done, can any of us ever accurately say, *This church is mine?* Can any of us say, *I paid for the church?* We can pay for a building and even for a budget, but we are using God's money to do it. Furthermore, none of us can ever duplicate Christ's perfect sacrifice for Christ's church.

Relevance for Today

In all things, we must defer to Christ's sovereignty and Lordship. There is no middle ground. Either

Christ is first, or we are first! Which is it? Jesus told his disciples in Matthew 6:33, "Seek ye first the kingdom of God" (KJV). Because Jesus is the firstborn creator and the firstborn resurrected one, let us give him glory!

We have been bought with a price. Let us glorify God with all that we are.

Jesus paid it all,
All to Him I owe;
Sin had left a crimson stain,
He wash'd it white as snow.[3]

Gnosticism

Who were Paul's opponents in Colosse? The letter gives us glimpses of the Gnosticism that plagued the early church. Gnostics prided themselves on their own elite understanding of God. The Gnostic view may have been part of the mixture of ideas that plagued the church at Colosse with a heretical understanding of the work of Christ. Gnosticism posited that an evil world could not have been created by a good God. Consequently, Gnostics attributed the creation to a long line of emanations from God culminating in Christ. Thus they diminished the work of Christ as Creator and distanced him from God.

Paul challenged the Gnostics' misunderstanding of Christ. In Colossians 1:19 and 2:9 Paul wrote that all of God filled Christ in the incarnation.

When believers receive Christ, therefore, we receive the fullness of God into our lives. A life filled with Christ fulfills God's purpose in the creation of the world.

Colosse

On a hill far away in present-day Turkey, my family and I stood in the Lycus Valley with a number of our church members. Laodicea was not far away, and neither was Hierapolis with its hot springs. At the bottom of the valley, one finds a large hill with a little stream running beside it. Archaeologists call it a *tel*. Beneath it lie the treasures of a Roman city, the thriving city of Colosse in the first century.

Questions

1. What practical difference can the supremacy of Christ make in our daily decisions?

2. How do you interpret Paul's assertion in 1:16 that all things were made by Christ and for Christ?

3. How do we incorporate the supremacy of Christ into the church's policies, procedures, and actions?

4. In what ways do you show that Christ is first in your life?

NOTES

1. Augustine, *Confessions*, I.1.
2. "The Church's One Foundation," words by Samuel J. Stone, 1866.
3. "Jesus Paid It All," words by Elvina M. Hall, 1865.

Main Idea

Life in Christ does not come from dependence on rituals and rulekeeping but from Christ himself, who is more than sufficient for our needs.

Question to Explore

What place do rituals and rules have in the Christian life?

LESSON
SEVEN

Lose the Rules

Study Aim

To evaluate the place rituals and rules have in my life and decide to rely fully on Christ

Study and Action Emphases

- Affirm the Bible as our authoritative guide for life and ministry
- Share the gospel with all people
- Develop a growing, vibrant faith
- Equip people for servant leadership

Quick Read

Is Jesus enough for us? Either his work on the cross made us right with God or it didn't. If we believe in Christ, and we are in Christ, then we have not only been forgiven, but we have been baptized into Christ's death, dying to the basic principles of the world, and we have been raised with Christ to a brand new life.

An elderly interim pastor wanted to reach out to the students in a small Southern community. He volunteered to help at the high school. He was surprised to receive his first assignment to be a chaperone at the school dance. When he arrived, he learned that his job was to keep the students in the dance and out of the cars in the parking lot.

On his very first watch, he saw two students in a car with steamed-up windows. When he knocked softly, the descending window revealed to his surprise that the two culprits were a boy and girl from the church he served. He smiled at them and invited them to leave the car and rejoin the dance. They smiled and said, "But Pastor, we are Baptists. We don't dance!" This simple story reminds us that we Baptists are all too often known for the things we do not do.

In the first-century city of Colosse, a group attempted to force the believers to conform to their own legalistic brand of religion. Like the Judaizers in the Galatian church, they sought to limit the freedom of the believers by forcing adherence to Jewish festival seasons and dietary laws. With their intense focus on returning to the Jewish law, they were hurting other believers in the name of God.

Unfortunately, legalism lives on to this day. If you have ever run into the scrutinizing eye of the legalist, you will never forget it. My first class in my second stint at Baylor University allowed me to study "Paul and the Law" under the tutelage of then professor Dr. Robert Sloan, who is now President of Baylor

University. I waded into an enormous task in my first paper, and I worked diligently. When I finished forty pages on the minute subject of the use of the Greek word *telos* in Romans 10:4, I mass-produced the paper and brought it to class. The first person to meet me took one look at the paper and said, "The final sigma nailed you." In horror, I realized that I had indeed used the wrong form for the Greek letter sigma in the whole paper. Crestfallen, I knew I would get an *F*. Because I had such reverence for Dr. Sloan, I dreaded him coming in and seeing my mistake.

I was experiencing the ugly sting of legalism. I was writing about Christ and the law, and a fellow student judged me as having failed to keep the laws of spelling. You would think that his criticism would have made me gracious to others. But for a while afterward, I became the proofreader of all proofreaders. I caught every misspelling, every missing comma. Grammatically, I was the careless student's worst nightmare. Because I had been caught I would catch others. Such legalism is like the West Nile virus. Once it works its way into our lives, it infiltrates our whole being. As much as we hate being judged, we become the judges of others.

Paul loved the church at Colosse. He loved them enough to labor for them to become perfect in Christ (see Colossians 1:28–29). This maturity, far from being measured in terms of legalistic righteousness, comes from being *in Christ*. For Paul either Christ sufficed as enough or he didn't. If Christ is enough, then no amount of legalism can add to Christ's perfect work of saving us.

Paul wrote the Colossians to say, *Christ is enough.* Since Christ judged the powers once and for all, we are no longer subject to them. Jesus liberates us from the condemnation of our would-be accusers.

Colossians 2:6–23

6As you therefore have received Christ Jesus the Lord, continue to live your lives in him, **7**rooted and built up in him and established in the faith, just as you were taught, abounding in thanksgiving.

8See to it that no one takes you captive through philosophy and empty deceit, according to human tradition, according to the elemental spirits of the universe, and not according to Christ. **9**For in him the whole fullness of deity dwells bodily, **10**and you have come to fullness in him, who is the head of every ruler and authority. **11**In him also you were circumcised with a spiritual circumcision, by putting off the body of the flesh in the circumcision of Christ; **12**when you were buried with him in baptism, you were also raised with him through faith in the power of God, who raised him from the dead. **13**And when you were dead in trespasses and the uncircumcision of your flesh, God made you alive together with him, when he forgave us all our trespasses, **14**erasing the record that stood against us with its legal demands. He set this aside, nailing it to the cross. **15**He disarmed the rulers and authorities and made a public example of them, triumphing over them in it.

16Therefore do not let anyone condemn you in matters of food and drink or of observing festivals, new moons, or sabbaths. **17**These are only a shadow of what is to come, but the substance belongs to Christ. **18**Do not let anyone disqualify you, insisting on self-abasement and worship of angels, dwelling on visions, puffed up without cause by a human way of thinking, **19**and not holding fast to the head, from whom the whole body, nourished and held together by its ligaments and sinews, grows with a growth that is from God.

20If with Christ you died to the elemental spirits of the universe, why do you live as if you still belonged to the world? Why do you submit to regulations, **21**"Do not handle, Do not taste, Do not touch"? **22**All these regulations refer to things that perish with use; they are simply human commands and teachings. **23**These have indeed an appearance of wisdom in promoting self-imposed piety, humility, and severe treatment of the body, but they are of no value in checking self-indulgence.

In Christ Resides the Fullness of God! (2:6–9)

The false teachers wreaked havoc at Colosse by claiming a higher wisdom. They told the believers in Colosse that there were some truths that only a few could understand. While claiming access to these truths, they sought to diminish Christ and judge the Christians.

First they tried to diminish Christ by distancing him from God (2:8–9). Claiming to comprehend mysteries, they would have said that since God is good and the world is evil, the creator of the world was evil. Since God could not touch evil, God sent out a progressive series of aeons or angelic messengers. Christ was the last messenger, and so Christ was far removed from God.

Jesus liberates us from the condemnation of our would-be accusers.

Paul said in 1:19, "God was pleased to have all his fullness dwell in him," referring to Christ. In 2:2, we learn that Christ is "the mystery of God" and in him "are hidden all the treasures of wisdom and knowledge." In 2:9, Paul wrote, "In Christ all the fullness of the Deity lives in bodily form."

So much bad theology today tries to diminish Christ. One of the warning signs of bad theology in any religious group is the diminution of Jesus, even to attempting to make Jesus merely a human being, ignoring Jesus' divinity.

In Christ, We Receive Everything We Need! (2:10–15)

In 2:5–6, we learn that we are saved when we believe and receive Christ as Lord. This, however, is not the end of the journey. In verses 6–7 we learn that believers grow in Christ as we "continue to live in him, rooted and built up in him, strengthened in the faith as you were taught."

We grow through good teaching as Christ fills us and gives us all we need. When we live in the Christ who is filled with the fullness of God, our lives are full as well.

Anyone who has ever used a computer spellchecker has seen some of the insane recommendations a spellchecker will make for seemingly common words that, for some reason, were not included in the checker's dictionary. A certain pastor was writing a column focusing on the need to lift up the name of Jesus in the marketplace. When he had finished typing the words into his word processor, he ran a spell check. The program stopped at the word "Jesus" with the comment, "Does not exist." It's true. Jesus does not exist in anybody's vocabulary until we intentionally put Jesus in. Is Jesus in our theological vocabulary? Unless we believe in Jesus and all that he did and that we are in him, our lives deteriorate quickly into a hypocritical legalism.

Christ utterly defeated any cosmic powers that seek to enslave human beings in a life of observing rituals and keeping rules.

Verses 10–15 emphasize that Jesus is enough, more than enough. These verses speak of the spiritual reality of what occurs in a person's relationship with

Christ. Rather than ritual, what God in Christ has done for us is what is important. It is in "the power of God" that we are "buried with him in baptism and raised with him" (2:12). Furthermore, Paul wrote the troubled Colossian church that it is God who "made you alive with Christ" (2:13).

Verses 13–14 stress the sufficiency of Christ in contrast to various attempts to add to or substitute for what Christ has done through keeping rituals and rules: "He forgave us all our sins, having canceled the written code, with its regulations, that was against us and that stood opposed to us; he took it away, nailing it to the cross."

If Christ is enough, then no amount of legalism can add to Christ's perfect work of saving us.

Verse 15 highlights the extent of Christ's victory: "Having disarmed the powers and authorities, he made a public spectacle of them, triumphing over them by the cross." Christ utterly defeated any cosmic powers that seek to enslave human beings in a life of observing rituals and keeping rules.

In Christ, Legalism Was Destroyed on the Cross (2:16–23)

The false teachers at Colosse endeavored to judge the believers (2:16, 20–23). Once the false teachers at Colosse had judged the head of the body—Christ— they began to judge the body of Christ itself.

The false teachers believed Christ was not enough for true salvation. Thus they set up rules that they believed were necessary to complete Christ's work. They said, *You have to be perfect like us, and you can do that by following these rules.* Paul countered, in effect (see 1:28–29), *The only way to be perfect is through Christ, and I am struggling to present you to God as perfect, mature, complete.*

The false teachers compared others to their inflated image of themselves. To please them, one had to eat and drink the right things (2:16, 21) and to keep the religious festivals and Sabbath days (2:16; see also 1 Chronicles 23:31; 2 Chronicles 2:4; 31:3; Nehemiah 10:33; Hosea 10:11). They had forgotten the teachings of Christ, who had said, "The sabbath was made for humankind, and not humankind for the sabbath" (Mark 2:27, NRSV).

In Colossians 2:15–17, we learn that since Christ has disarmed the powers and authorities, we are no longer to be judged by them. The Sabbath and dietary laws are the shadow, but Christ is the reality. Furthermore, when we attempt to add observing rituals and keeping rules to what Christ has done for us, we err greatly

> When we live in the Christ who is filled with the fullness of God, our lives are full as well.

and are "not holding fast to the head" (2:19, NASB), referring to Christ himself. Those who observe rituals and keep rules to supplement Christ have lost touch with Christ.

In my first pastorate in rural Texas, an elderly deacon invited me to his home for lunch. While we sat in his living room, I could sense he was struggling with something. I invited him to explain. Pointing to the cows in the pasture next to his house, he said, "I tried to get my cows to come up into the pasture all day yesterday to no avail. Right now they are all up. If I went and closed the gate, my work for tomorrow would be done. But then I would be working on the Sabbath."

I tried to be sensitive to his conscience on that matter. Still, I told him I was convinced that Jesus would have said, *Go and close the gate!*

Paul had already shown that Christ's death on the cross cancelled the written code with its regulations (2:14–15). The legalists in Colosse had put their human spin on God's commands and created an elaborate system by which to enforce their casuistry. The forces of evil in the world had co-opted these legalists' efforts and created a new bondage for the believers.

This simple story reminds us that we Baptists are all too often known for the things we do not do.

Christ, though, had triumphed over the powers of evil on the cross and made a public display in a triumphal procession over his enemies through the resurrection. Christ's resurrection confirmed the defeat of Satan and his minions. They no longer rule. So Christ, who is more than enough, has disposed of legalistic rules.

In the end, such rules do not accomplish what they intend anyway. Have you ever seen a sign that said, *Do not touch this*? What did it make you want to do? After God had said to humankind, *Don't eat the fruit from the tree of knowledge of good and evil* (Genesis 2:15–17), Satan tempted Adam and Eve so that they saw the fruit and wanted it.

> Those who observe rituals and keep rules to supplement Christ have lost touch with Christ.

Some years ago, while studying for a week at a seminary, I ate in the cafeteria. At the front of the serving line was a large pile of oranges. Somebody posted a note: "Take only one; God is watching." At the other end of the table was a large pile of chocolate chip cookies. One of the students had written a note: "Take all you want; God is watching the oranges."

Of course, Christ sees all. Since he holds our lives in his hands, what will he do? I return to my story of the typographic errors in my first paper in my graduate studies at Baylor University. The professor entered the room as I sat there embarrassed and ashamed. In the presence of my peers he said, "This is a very fine paper." He never mentioned the hundreds of typos on the same word. In his gracious kindness, he showed me the spirit of Paul's teaching.

Relevance for Today

We are not ultimately judged on the darkness of our many mistakes, but in the resplendent grace of God.

The law and legalism could never save. But what the law could not do, Christ has already done.

The hymn writer captured the thought well:[1]

Free from the law, O happy condition,
Jesus hath bled, and there is remission;
Cursed by the law and bruised by the fall,
Grace hath redeemed us once for all.

Legalism

Paul referred to the "basic principles" in Colossians 2:8, 20. The Greek word is *stoicheia*. Other translations include "elemental spirits" (NRSV) and "elementary principles" (NASB).

The Colossian legalists used these elementary *ABCs* of legalism to bind the early believers. Paul identified this practice as hollow and deceptive philosophy that encouraged dependence on human tradition instead of on Christ.

How do we as believers respond to legalism? Paul suggested we have a funeral. We must die with Christ to such legalism (2:20).

Once in a rural church, I had a friend who would not eat catfish because of the Old Testament definition of appropriate fish having scales and fins (see Leviticus 11:9–12). This friend loved catfish, however. One day we were fishing for trout, and I caught a catfish. Immediately he suggested that I could not ever eat the fish because it was "unclean." I joyfully showed him Peter's experience in Acts 10:9–16. In that experience God showed Peter that people were liberated from the petty legalities of the Jewish dietary, ritual, and ceremonial laws.

The people of God are to live in the clear light of the New Testament. We are free indeed.

Questions

1. What evidence of legalism do you see in the church today?
2. Has the judgmentalism of others ever infected you, leading you to judge? How do we apply Jesus' teaching in Matthew 7:1 on judging?
3. Have you appropriated Paul's teaching in Colossians 2:9–10? How is your life richer and fuller because of Christ?
4. How can we as believers show the love of Christ to both the legalists and the people whom they oppress?
5. In what ways do Christians tend to rely on and give more attention to rituals and rules—*do's* and *don'ts, oughts* and *shoulds*—than to Christ?

NOTES

1. Free from the "Law, O Happy Condition," words by Philip P. Bliss, 1873.

Focal Text

Colossians
3:1—4:1

Background

Colossians
3:1—4:6

Main Idea

Christians are to live
lives that reflect that Christ
himself is their life.

Question to Explore

How should our faith
affect our lives?

LESSON
EIGHT

Live It Up!

Study Aim

To summarize Paul's teachings about Christian living and identify at least one way I will apply these teachings

Study and Action Emphases

- Affirm the Bible as our authoritative guide for life and ministry
- Share the gospel with all people
- Develop a growing, vibrant faith
- Value all people as created in the image of God
- Encourage healthy families
- Equip people for servant leadership

Quick Read

How do believers live moral lives without being moralistic? Is it possible to be holy without being holier than thou? For believers, Christ embodies the single absolute reality. He is all and in all. Since in Christ we live and move and have our being, in Christ alone do we discover the power to live resurrected lives.

The story is told of a mother whose seven children went out to play. As the kids enjoyed a vigorous game of hide and seek near the apartment complex where they lived, roofers were putting new tar on the roof. During the course of the game, the youngest child thought it might be a good idea to hide in a half empty barrel of the tar. Fortunately, the tar wasn't hot enough to harm the child, but when he emerged he was covered in it. When the older children brought the tar-covered youngster back to his mother, she looked him up and down all covered in tar and said, "Boy, it would be easier to make another one than to clean you up." God has done precisely that in salvation. In Christ, God not only cleanses us, but God also re-creates us.

With a full recognition of this new creation, Paul challenged the Colossian believers to live up to their position in Christ. Some speak of Christians who are so heavenly minded that they are no earthly good. Paul was more concerned about Christians who were so earthly minded that they were little heavenly good. So Paul admonished them, "Set your minds on things above" (Colossians 3:2).

How do believers live moral lives without being moralistic? Is it possible to be holy without being holier than thou? For Paul, Christ embodied the single absolute reality. He is all and in all. In Christ alone do we discover the power to live resurrected lives. It takes Christ's resurrection power working in believers to transform us from sinful people into

God's chosen people who are holy, humble, compassionate, kind, gentle, and patient. In his Letter to the Colossians, Paul reminded the believers that life in Christ entails joining Christ in his death, burial, and resurrection. Paul encouraged the believers in Colosse to put to death their sinful earthly natures. Then just as Christ arose, believers were to clothe themselves in the new clothes of the resurrection in true righteousness.

Colossians 3:1—4:1

1So if you have been raised with Christ, seek the things that are above, where Christ is, seated at the right hand of God. **2**Set your minds on things that are above, not on things that are on earth, **3**for you have died, and your life is hidden with Christ in God. **4**When Christ who is your life is revealed, then you also will be revealed with him in glory.

5Put to death, therefore, whatever in you is earthly: fornication, impurity, passion, evil desire, and greed (which is idolatry). **6**On account of these the wrath of God is coming on those who are disobedient. **7**These are the ways you also once followed, when you were living that life. **8**But now you must get rid of all such things—anger, wrath, malice, slander, and abusive language from your mouth. **9**Do not lie to one another, seeing that you have stripped off the old self with its practices **10**and have clothed yourselves with the new self, which is being renewed in knowledge according to the image of its creator. **11**In that renewal there is no longer Greek and Jew, circumcised and uncircumcised, barbarian, Scythian, slave and free; but Christ is all and in all!

12As God's chosen ones, holy and beloved, clothe yourselves with compassion, kindness, humility, meekness, and patience. **13**Bear with one another and, if anyone has a complaint against another, forgive each other; just as the Lord has forgiven you, so you also must forgive. **14**Above all, clothe yourselves with love, which binds everything together in perfect harmony. **15**And let the peace of Christ rule in your hearts, to which indeed you were called in the one body. And be thankful. **16**Let the word of Christ dwell in you richly; teach and admonish one another in all wisdom; and with gratitude in your hearts sing psalms, hymns, and spiritual songs to God. **17**And whatever you do, in word or deed, do everything in the name of the Lord Jesus, giving thanks to God the Father through him.

18Wives, be subject to your husbands, as is fitting in the Lord. **19**Husbands, love your wives and never treat them harshly.

20Children, obey your parents in everything, for this is your acceptable duty in the Lord. **21**Fathers, do not provoke your children, or they may lose heart. **22**Slaves, obey your earthly masters in everything, not only while being watched and in order to please them, but wholeheartedly, fearing the Lord. **23**Whatever your task, put yourselves into it, as done for the Lord and not for your masters, **24**since you know that from the Lord you will receive the inheritance as your reward; you serve the Lord Christ. **25**For the wrongdoer will be paid back for whatever wrong has been done, and there is no partiality. **4:1**Masters, treat your slaves justly and fairly, for you know that you also have a Master in heaven.

What to Dispose Of (3:1–9)

In verses 1–9, Paul stated that in Christ, believers dispose of the old wardrobe of sin. They do this, Paul reminded them, because true believers have "died" (3:3). Earlier Paul had argued that they had died to the *stoicheia*—the demonically empowered principles of this world (2:20; see article, "Legalism," in lesson seven). Consequently, they no longer lived under the legalism that would perish with the world. In 3:3 he reiterated, "For you died." Then

> . . . Paul challenged the Colossian believers to live up to their position in Christ.

in verse 5 Paul reminded them that if they had died to sin, then they needed to put sinful behavior to death. These sins brought the wrath of God, according to verse 6. Again, in verse 7 Paul said that the Colossians used to live lives of sin. Now, though, in Christ, things were to be different (3:8–14).

In John 11:44, when Lazarus came forth from the tomb, Jesus said, "Take off the grave clothes and let him go." He was saying that grave clothes are for the dead. The friends of Lazarus were to take off his grave clothes and clothe him in the clothes of the living.

The day we receive Christ, we don't just become members of a local church, and we don't just say to ourselves that we'll try harder to do better. The day we are saved, the Spirit of the Holy God comes to live inside us, and we cross over from death to life (John 5:24).

Thus, believers are to put sexual sin to death! In four Greek expressions in verse 5, Paul covered the bases of sexual sin. First Paul used the word translated "sexual immorality," which is the Greek word that gives us the English word *pornography*. Paul then named "impurity, lust," and "evil desires." Notice that Paul did not condemn the physical desires or sensuality within mar-

> *Anything we worship other than God usurps the unique place of God in our lives.*

riage. Rather, these terms refer to the distortion of those desires by twisting them into something God did not intend. God does not disallow or deny the fact that he created human beings as sexual creatures. Instead, Paul disallowed the sinful choices that would distort God's good gifts to us.

Further, believers are to put greed to death. In a materialistic culture, we might be reluctant to include greed on this list of sins. Nevertheless, Paul equated greed with idolatry. Anything we worship other than God usurps the unique place of God in our lives.

Ecclesiastes 5:10 reminds us, "Whoever loves money never has money enough; whoever loves wealth is never satisfied with his income. This too is meaningless." How often the things we aspire to possess ultimately possess us!

Paul didn't stop with the prohibitions, though, and neither does Christianity.

Believers also are to put sins of anger to death (Col. 3:8). Of the five negative behaviors in verse 8, the first three relate pointedly to anger, with the last two including negative expressions in speech.

What makes you angry? A small girl was showing a friend the bathroom scale. She said, "I don't know what it is, but my mom and dad use it every day. All I know is, when you stand on it, it makes you really mad!" In an age of rage, believers demonstrate the power of Christ through self-control.

The monks at a remote monastery deep in the forest followed a rigid vow of silence. Their vow could be broken only once a year—on Christmas—by one monk. That monk could speak only one sentence. One Christmas, Brother Thomas had his turn to speak and said, "I love the delightful mashed potatoes we have every year with the Christmas roast!" Then he sat down. Silence ensued for 365 days. The next Christmas, Brother Michael got his turn and said, "I think the mashed potatoes are lumpy, and I truly despise them!" Once again, silence ensued for 365 days. The following Christmas, Brother Paul rose and said, "I am fed up with this constant bickering!"

To be pleasing to God, we must deal summarily and ruthlessly with our anger and our bitterness against others. In addition, believers are to put to death the sin of dishonesty. The business scandals of recent times reveal the prevalence of this sin in our world.

If I refuse to forgive you, then I am actually insisting that you must pay for your failure again and again and again.

All of these prohibitions may make it sound to some that true Christianity is about a bunch of negative rules. Paul didn't stop with the prohibitions, though, and neither does Christianity. Not only do we let sinful attitudes and actions die, but we become new. We throw away our grave clothes and put on a new wardrobe.

What to Put On (3:10–17)

In Colossians 1:15, Paul told the believers that Jesus is the image of God. In 3:10 we learn that believers become like Christ as they are renewed in the image of God. This transformation is progressive (2 Corinthians 3:18), but it will be complete in the end (1 John 3:2). The believer's new self is renewed in knowledge in the image of his Creator. Accordingly, the One who created the world and is responsible for our lives wants to recreate us. This time, however, he wants us to fulfill his design for creation. What is that? The design is that we become like Christ and live in fellowship with the Creator.

Note that we are chosen for new life regardless of human distinctions and differences (Col. 3:11). So much animosity in our world revolves around ethnicity, education, and economics. Christ transcends all of those differences. Sometimes we come to the church with a different agenda than that of focusing on Christ. We wrap up our religion with our politics or with our plan to make money. As a result our personal agenda usurps the place of our commitment to Christ. Let it not be so in the church! Christ is all and in all!

. . . When the time came for the Lord's Supper, a Japanese Christian brought him the bread and the cup, and fellowship was created at the foot of the cross.

We are to clothe ourselves with the clothing of Christ and to become compassionate, kind, humble, gentle, and patient (3:12). Christ was kind. We misrepresent Christ to the world when we are unkind to others.

Recently, my friend Vaiden Dozier passed away. Vaiden consistently portrayed the kindness of Christ in all of his relationships. In my preparation for the funeral, I realized that Vaiden was the way he was because God is the way God is. When we become followers of Christ, in time we take on Christ's character.

Likewise, we are to forgive because God is a forgiving God and we have been forgiven (3:13).

Refusing to forgive someone is our attempt to maintain control over that person. If I refuse to forgive you, then I am actually insisting that you must pay for your failure again and again and again.

Buckner Fanning, the longtime pastor of Trinity Baptist Church in San Antonio, went to Japan just after World War II as a soldier. When he arrived there, he saw the devastation caused by the bombs dropped there. Looking for a place to worship, he found a Japanese Christian church, a small room with folding chairs and a table up in front with the communion elements on it. As a United States Marine, he wondered how the Japanese people might feel about him. At first, they seemed distant and cold. But when the time came for the Lord's Supper, a Japanese Christian brought him the bread and the cup, and fellowship was created at the foot of the cross. The cross restores fellowship with God and with one another.

> *Mature Christians sacrifice their own desires and agendas for the sake of worshiping God.*

Most of all, Paul said, we are to put on love (3:14). Love is the belt that makes the whole outfit work. As I left the hospital after a visit recently, I walked toward my car and thought about all that God has given me—not in terms of material possessions but in terms of love from family and friends. Love binds "together in perfect unity" all the virtues Paul described (3:14).

Believers are to clothe themselves in the joy of the Lord. In 3:15–17, we learn that Christ fills our hearts with his praise in songs of joy and thanksgiving. Such music draws people together. Astonishingly, many churches divide over the issue of music. Gratitude and unity undergird Paul's teachings in this passage. So God's people express gratitude to God in the music we sing. Mature Christians sacrifice their own desires and agendas for the sake of worshiping God.

How to Live at Home and Work (3:18—4:1)

What is the single most essential ingredient in the home? Paul would respond, *relationship with the Lord Jesus Christ*. In this section about life in the household, Paul discussed relationships between husbands and wives, parents and children, and slaves and masters. Of course, Paul wrote to people in an ancient world where society considered women to be chattel with no rights and where masters possessed a despotic power over their slaves. We must not ignore those cultural conditions as we study these verses.

How shall we interpret these instructions today? These specific teachings make little sense for us apart from the total context, especially verse 17. Why would husbands and wives submit to each other unless it is as to the Lord? Why would we love, obey, or nurture, apart from the Lord? In the reciprocal relationships of families, each person must work on his or her own weakness to strengthen the home. We do this not primarily because of the worthiness of the other person in the relationship but because of the worthiness of Christ. In the presence of the Lord, answering to him in all of our relationships, we are to love our spouses, raise our children, obey our parents, and relate to our employers and employees. God is not only the silent witness in these relationships, but God also is the ultimate judge to whom we will give an account.

In our work relationships we are to do what we do for God.

The wife submits her strengths to the husband as to Christ, while the husband lives in submission to the same Lord. The husband must not devalue or denigrate the wife. When both husband and wife submit as children of God, no power struggle ensues. Why not? Both husband and wife know that the Lord is in charge. In Ephesians 5:21, we see this as mutual submission out of reverence for Christ.

When a wife submits to a husband or a husband to his wife, neither is saying that the other is always right, but rather that in love they will care first about the needs of the other. My wife Melanie has never allowed me to mistake her quietness for weakness. Actually, her quiet strength and dignity empower her to relate to me without harping or criticizing, even though I am often in error.

The husband must learn to love in the Lord; "Husbands, love your wives." How do we do it? Ephesians 5:25 challenges, "As Christ loved the church . . . ." How did Christ do that? By laying down his life.

All air travelers have heard the flight attendant repeat the familiar line, "If you are traveling with small children, in the event of the loss of cabin pressure, first place the mask on your own face, and then place the mask on your child's face." In family life, parents sometimes spend most of their time placing oxygen masks on their children's faces while the marriage relationship suffocates. The only way to have a strong family is to make sure that husband and wife keep the oxygen supply of love flowing strong between them.

In the second reciprocal relationship, parents encourage and children obey. Notice once again the balance. God established the relationship for the protection and nurture of children. Thus parents are to discipline without discouraging.

Regardless of our positions or responsibilities, we all answer to the ultimate Boss, God.

In the final reciprocal relationship, slaves are to obey as masters provide. The slave-master relationship was a relationship within the Roman household of that day. The employee-employer relationship provides the best parallel today. The details of 3:22—4:1 are to be carried out in the context of 3:17: "Whatever you do, in word or deed, do it all in the name of the Lord Jesus. . . ." In our work relationships we are to do what we do for God.

Employees are to obey, not to please others super-ficially but to please God sincerely. Employers are to provide what is right and fair for employees. Regard-less of our positions or responsibilities, we all answer to the ultimate Boss, God.

A New Beginning

One week in July 2002, Tallowood Baptist Church of Houston, Texas, sent students on mission trips to five destinations. In Recife, Brazil, the group went to a church at the dump and discovered that people live there. In fact, the children have plenty of things to play with—from the dump. They even have clothes to wear and food to eat—from the dump. Sometimes the truck drivers who drop off the trash abuse the children.

The government of Brazil attempted to fix the prob-lem by building new homes for all the "dump people." But the former dump residents sold these homes and moved back to the dump. The pastor of the church said, "You can take the people out of the rubbish, but it is much harder to get the rubbish out of the people."

How do we get the rubbish out of the people? Fill them with Christ. The government can't do it. Who can do it? Jesus can, and he is transforming lives there. In the middle of that community is a church called *Agua Vida*—the "water of life" church. In the vital worship of that church, many of the residents have exchanged a life of refuse and rubbish for a new beginning.

Questions

1. What difference should the resurrection of Christ make in the way we live? (See 3:1–3.)

2. How should our relationship with Christ affect our relationships with people of different cultures, races, or economic levels? (See 3:11.)

3. In a practical way, how might your church extend hands across the human differences that so often divide?

4. What old attitudes or actions do you need to leave behind as you immerse your life in the presence and power of the risen Lord? (See 3:5–9.)

5. What new practices do you need to take up? (See 3:10–17.)

6. In what ways do your actions at work represent the Lordship of Christ?

Introducing

1 AND 2 THESSALONIANS: Faith, Love, and Hope

The two New Testament letters to the Christians at Thessalonica reveal the pastoral heart of Paul the missionary. He and the missionary leadership team had established the church at Thessalonica in the Roman province of Macedonia, the same province as Philippi, near the midpoint of the first century AD (see Acts 17:1–9). According to Acts, after spending only a brief time there, the leadership team had left the city and continued the missionary efforts in Berea, Athens, and Corinth. Out of pastoral concern for the Thessalonian Christians and a desire to provide them further instructions on some questions they had, Paul wrote back to them. The result is our two New Testament letters, 1 and 2 Thessalonians.

First Thessalonians is the oldest letter of Paul, having been written about 50 AD. Mark, the first of the four gospels to be written down, did not appear until the mid–60s. The Book of James may be the oldest New Testament book, perhaps written as early as 48 AD, but it is also possible that 1 Thessalonians itself is the very earliest New Testament book to have been written.

First and Second Thessalonians resemble each other in structure, and each contains some elements that remind us of the other. In each letter, Paul began by giving thanks for the church at Thessalonica. In the first lesson on 1 Thessalonians, which is lesson nine in this issue, we will study the sort of church it was and seek to discover qualities we can apply to our own churches (1 Thessalonians 1:1–10; 2:13–20; 3:1–13; 2 Thess. 1:1–4).

Especially in 1 Thessalonians, Paul described the way in which he and the missionary team sought to give leadership to the Thessalonians. The second lesson on 1 Thessalonians looks at the qualities of leadership that Paul commended and the missionary team demonstrated (1 Thess. 2:1–12; 5:12–13). This lesson will call us to consider the kind of leadership we ourselves value.

The third lesson focuses on the ways in which the Thessalonian Christians were to live so as to please God (1 Thess. 4:1–12; 5:14–21). This lesson will challenge us to measure our lives by these qualities.

The fourth lesson treats a theme that appears in both letters—the Christian hope and the return of Christ (1 Thess. 4:13—5:11; 2 Thess. 1:5—2:12). Much space is given in each letter to this theme. Our study will emphasize the treatment of this theme in 1 Thessalonians. This passage, particularly 4:13–18, has long been the source of great help to Christians who have lost loved ones. As we study the Christian hope in this lesson, the message for the Thessalonian Christians and for us is to "encourage each other with these words" (1 Thess. 4:18), rather than to fear or ignore them.[1] Studying this passage can enable us to learn to deal in a Christian manner with death—the death of our loved ones and, lest we forget, of ourselves.

The final lesson deals with a problem that appears in both letters—the failure on the part of some of the Thessalonians to express their Christian faith in their daily work (2 Thess. 3:6–13). They simply did not work, evidently expecting others to support them. This lesson gives us an opportunity to consider how we ourselves live out our faith in an area we often neglect—our daily work.

1 AND 2 THESSALONIANS: FAITH, LOVE, AND HOPE

Additional Resources for Studying 1 and 2 Thessalonians:[2]

F.F. Bruce. *1 & 2 Thessalonians*. Word Biblical Commentary. Volume 45. Waco, Texas: Word Books, Inc., 1982.

Gary W. Demarest. *1, 2 Thessalonians; 1, 2 Timothy; and Titus.* The Comunicator's Commentary. Volume 9. Waco, TX: Word Books, Inc., 1984.

Beverly Roberts Gaventa. *First and Second Thessalonians.* Interpretation: A Bible Commentary for Teaching and Preaching. Louisville: John Knox Press, 1998.

Herschel H. Hobbs. "1—2 Thessalonians." *The Broadman Bible Commentary*. Volume 11. Nashville, Tennessee: Broadman Press, 1971.

Leon Morris. *The First and Second Epistles to the Thessalonians.* The New International Commentary on the New Testament. Grand Rapids, Michigan: Eerdmans, 1959, 1982.

A.T. Robertson. *Word Pictures in the New Testament.* Volume IV, The Epistles of Paul. Nashville, Tennessee: Broadman Press, 1931.

Abraham Smith. "The First Letter to the Thessalonians" and "The Second Letter to the Thessalonians." *The New Interpreter's Bible*. Volume XI. Nashville: Abingdon Press, 2000.

NOTES

1. Unless otherwise indicated, all Scripture quotations in this
    introduction and the lessons on 1 and 2 Thessalonians are
    from the New International Version.
2. Listing a book does not imply full agreement by the writers or
    BAPTISTWAY PRESS® with all of its comments.

Focal Text

1 Thessalonians
1:1–10; 2:13–14

Background

1 Thessalonians
1:1–10; 2:13–20;
3:1–13;
2 Thessalonians
1:1–4

Main Idea

A church for which to be grateful shows its faithfulness to the gospel through demonstrating its faith, hope, and love.

Question to Explore

What about your church makes you grateful?

LESSON NINE

A Church for Which to Be Grateful

Study Aim

To identify marks of a church for which to be grateful and evaluate how well our church shows them

Study and Action Emphases

- Affirm the Bible as our authoritative guide for life and ministry
- Share the gospel with all people
- Develop a growing, vibrant faith
- Include all God's family in decision-making and service
- Value all people as created in the image of God
- Encourage healthy families
- Obey and serve Jesus by meeting physical, spiritual, and emotional needs
- Equip people for servant leadership

Quick Read

By faithfully embodying the essence of Christ dwelling in human lives, faithful churches give testimony to the continuing reality of the work of the Holy Spirit.

Some years ago my wife came up with a most meaningful Christmas gift for me. Rummaging through years of photographs, she found snapshots of buildings of all the churches we had served through nearly four decades of ministry. An artist friend then did pen-and-ink drawings of each. We framed them as reminders of our ministry experiences. You can imagine that these pictures are much more than just art work for the walls of my study. These drawings prompt us to reflect on the experiences of seven periods of ministry.

Needless to say, our church experience has been more than buildings. Church life is about people. In our family's church experiences over the years, there are people who stand out in our memories because of their marvelous example of Christian devotion, maturity, and integrity. They influenced our lives, helped mold our children, and shaped our ministry. Those seven churches will always linger in our minds as significant expressions of our faith and our efforts to serve in ministry in response to God's call on our lives.

The centrality of churches in the story of an emerging Christianity in the New Testament cannot be overstated. Jesus clearly envisioned not isolated believers but a called-out people of God to continue his mission and message. He must have known that these expressions of God's people on earth would be imperfect reflections of the kingdom of God. Nevertheless, Jesus saw his task as incomplete until he had begun to bring together the roots of what would become congregations of believers.

Paul's epistles, among the first of the New Testament documents to be written, reflect his loving relationship with many churches. They relate his joy over their successes and his pastoral concern for their failures. Paul could look back on his experience with the churches he helped establish and see the qualities that had been the most effective and impressive.

To think of Christianity without the centrality of a visible and dynamic body of believers would be unthinkable from the vantage point of the New Testament. Christianity and the church are inseparable for an effective witness to the world of the transforming power of the risen Lord. Our studies in 1 and 2 Thessalonians will show us ways in which churches have embodied the best of the Christian way, ways in which we can enhance our churches in the twenty-first century.

1 Thessalonians 1:1–10

1Paul, Silas and Timothy,

To the church of the Thessalonians in God the Father and the Lord Jesus Christ:

Grace and peace to you.

2We always thank God for all of you, mentioning you in our prayers. **3**We continually remember before our God and Father your work produced by faith, your labor prompted by love, and your endurance inspired by hope in our Lord Jesus Christ.

4For we know, brothers loved by God, that he has chosen you, **5**because our gospel came to you not simply with words, but also with power, with the Holy Spirit and with deep conviction. You know how we lived among you for your sake. **6**You became imitators of us and of the Lord; in spite of severe suffering, you welcomed the message with the joy given by the Holy Spirit. **7**And so you became a model to all the believers in Macedonia and Achaia. **8**The Lord's message rang out from you not only in Macedonia and Achaia—your faith in God has become known everywhere. Therefore we do not need to say anything about it, **9**for they themselves report what kind of reception you gave us. They tell how you turned to God from idols to serve the living and true God, **10**and to wait for his Son from heaven, whom he raised from the dead—Jesus, who rescues us from the coming wrath.

1 Thessalonians 2:13–14

13And we also thank God continually because, when you received the word of God, which you heard from us, you accepted it not as the word of men, but as it actually is, the word of God, which is at work in you who believe. **14**For you, brothers, became imitators of God's churches in Judea, which are in Christ Jesus: You suffered from your own countrymen the same things those churches suffered from the Jews. . . .

Thessalonica—the City and Its Culture

Thessalonica was not only the largest and most important city of Macedonia, but it was also the capital of the province. Strategically located on the warm waters of the Thermaic Gulf, Thessalonica was a city with a rich history and great significance due to its location on the *Via Egnatia*, the principal trade route from Rome to the eastern provinces of the Roman Empire. Trade from east and west flowed through its streets and into ships in its port. This city was well known because of its size and wealth, its freedom from Roman interference, and its cosmopolitan population. It was to become the location of a marvelous story of effective church planting.

Church life is about people.

Thessalonica offered its people a religious smorgasbord. We learn from the text in Acts 17:1–13 that there was a Jewish community at Thessalonica. This Jewish community was large enough to support an active synagogue where Paul would go and teach. There was also a strong presence of Greek cults and various philosophies. Archeologists have found evidence of a number of other cults and religious groups in the city. Devotion to the Roman emperor ran deep in the minds of many. Coins minted in Thessalonica declaring Caesar to be divine have been found. With people and ideas from many places in the world moving in and through Thessalonica, one might wonder how the claims of the traveling Christian evangelists would be received.

Christianity came to the city with the witness of Paul and Silas. Acts 17:1–9 tells the story of the beginnings of this church. We read the account there of the brief visit to Thessalonica by Paul and his associates on the second of Paul's missionary journeys. Forced to leave Philippi by hostile crowds of skeptics, the determined missionaries made their way to this port city.

Our studies in 1 and 2 Thessalonians will show us ways in which churches have embodied the best of the Christian way, ways in which we can enhance our churches in the twenty-first century.

As was his custom, Paul went to the synagogue, which afforded an opportunity for the missionaries to speak their witness for Jesus as the Christ of God. The Acts account tells us that almost immediately Jews, "God-fearing Greeks" (Greeks who worshiped God but who had not become full-fledged Jews), and a sizeable number of women became believers (Acts 17:4). The response of the people and the establishment of a church in a short period of time provide a remarkable example of first-century evangelism and church growth.

Hardly had Paul begun to see this little congregation emerge when opposition began to be directed toward the group. No doubt enraged by the impact of the gospel on the lives of many people, some of the Jews and others they gathered began an uproar that threatened the peace of their community. They accused Paul and the believers of seeking to "cause trouble all over the world" (Acts 17:6). The disturbance resulted in Paul and Silas once again being sent out of a town to which they had brought the good news. In the cover of darkness, some of the believers escorted their friends out of the city and sent them on their way toward Berea.

The concern of Paul for this fledgling congregation must have run deep. With so little time to instruct them in their new faith, could they endure on their own? What about their ability to withstand the opposition and persecution that might well follow? What about their questions related to Paul's sudden departure? Would they understand that he had not intentionally deserted their cause?

The concern of Paul for this fledgling congregation must have run deep.

To answer these questions, Paul sent his trusted friend, Timothy, to return and visit the church to determine its status (see 1 Thess. 3:2–10). One can only imagine the joy and gratitude Paul must have felt when the word came back about the Thessalonian church. We cannot know in detail the report brought back by Timothy, but from the tone of Paul's two letters to the Thessalonians, we can glean much of the essence of what he found. These letters, very similar in many respects, show his joy and thanksgiving.

A Missionary's Prayer of Thanksgiving (1:1–5)

Paul began his letter with appreciation and thanksgiving for this young congregation, which had been thrust so soon into conflict with their culture and without the benefit of experienced leaders. Paul's prayer for this church was one of thanksgiving for the obvious strength of character that had emerged. This expression of thanks is repeated in 2:13 and 3:9.

Anyone who has been part of a new church start can identify with some of the hopes and fears that accompany such an effort.

The young son of a prominent preacher asked at lunch one Sunday, "Dad, when you preach, why are you always so angry?" Taken aback, the pastor was forced to listen to himself. He found that, indeed, his emphasis had often been more on criticism of his congregation's faults than praise for their victories. How different was the Apostle Paul's approach!

Paul began this letter with appreciation and praise for the church at Thessalonica. Verse 3 outlines three areas in which their Christian commitment was so evident. There was a "work produced by faith," a "labor prompted by love," and an "endurance inspired by hope" (1 Thess. 1:3).

Here we come face to face with three of Paul's great ideas of the Christian way. Faith, hope, and love are a trilogy of realities from which true Christianity flows. (See this trilogy of faith, hope, and love also in Romans 5:1–5; 1 Corinthians 13:13; Galatians 5:5–6; Colossians 1:4–5.) No doubt these three concepts formed much of Paul's instruction to the church at Thessalonica when he was there briefly in its earliest days.

Faith is the assurance that God was at work in Christ for the salvation of his people. Love is an active word describing the living out of the faith in dealing with one another. Hope is the confidence that what God has begun through Christ will lead Christians through the trials to ultimate victory in Christ.

As the Apostle pondered these realities, so evident in the life of the church at Thessalonica, he was moved to thanksgiving. He saw in these and other expressions of their faithfulness that he would mention later, that the Thessalonians truly had received the gospel. Not in mere words but in the evident presence of the Holy Spirit, they had moved out in faith (1 Thess. 1:5).

In verse 4 Paul addressed the believers with the term "brothers." We should not limit this to the male members of the congregation. As the New Revised Standard Version puts it, "brothers and sisters" is an appropriate description of those to whom the letter is addressed. Acts 17:4 does remind us that a good many "prominent women" were among the early converts.

A Church Planter's Dream (1:6–10)

The hope of church planters is that those churches will mature, reaching out to others in compassion, evangelism, and ministry. The planter dreams of a day when the little core of people who meet in a home or other such settings will one day be able to stand on their own as an expression of the People of God. Anyone who has been part of a new church start can identify with some of the hopes and fears that accompany such an effort. As the group passes through various challenges, there is often a mix of hope and anxiety, celebration and fear.

Paul and Silas must have had that kind of dream when they began to gather a cluster of believers in Thessalonica. They may have had some of the same concerns. Only time would tell the outcome, and now that time had come. Timothy's report could only bring excitement and a sense of fulfillment to what had once been only a vision.

The Thessalonian letters remind us of the difficulty for Christians living in the first century. They also provide us with the marvelous testimony of the faithfulness and courage of so many.

Among the problems they must have faced daily were these: (1) strong criticism and physical threats from some of the Jews; (2) temptations growing out of their background in a pagan culture; (3) lack of experience and limited examples of Christian doctrine and behavior from other Christians and their churches; (4)

misunderstandings by non-Christian neighbors, and (5) confusion over the anticipated return of Christ. Paul and Silas must have spent much time trying to prepare the new believers for any eventuality (2:10–12). Had these new Christians understood? Would they be ready when the testing came?

. . . The way people handle adversity reveals much about their faith.

Facing these and other pressing issues, this resolute band of young believers became a thrilling example for Paul, Silas, and Timothy. Indeed, word of their exemplary faith spread throughout Macedonia and Achaia, and regions beyond (1:8).

Suffering Servants (2:13–14)

Through suffering, the Thessalonian Christians had become one with other churches that had suffered (2:14). The church at Thessalonica was a young congregation and had neither met nor conversed with the scattered churches. Still, the Thessalonian church demonstrated their common life with fellow churches through the experiences of suffering. Paul affirmed them in this experience, attributing their faithfulness to their reliance on the gospel as "the word of God," and not on the speculations or hypotheses of pagan religions and philosophies (2:13).

Faithfulness quite often seems to bring opposition and challenges for those who follow Christ.

Much of the Christian world has recoiled at the suffering of fellow Christians in cultures around the world where their faith has cost them dearly in recent months. We have been moved by stories of missionaries killed, church buildings burned, and families separated. Even in our own experience, we may have felt some of the pain of being misunderstood, ridiculed, or pitied as people of faith in a secular culture.

On the other hand, the way people handle adversity reveals much about their faith. I remember as a young minister sitting with a faithful church member the night before a very serious surgery. I had tried to bring some encouragement to him, but I felt terribly inadequate. It was then that he ministered to me by saying, "Pastor, I don't know how this surgery is going, but however it goes, it's okay. I know that God is with me wherever I find myself tomorrow." That lesson in confidence in the face of trials was, and still is, a reminder of an important principle of the Christian life. I repeat that principle: how we handle adversity reveals much about our faith.

Faithfulness quite often seems to bring opposition and challenges for those who follow Christ.

Paul would have his friends understand that their suffering was not finished. When one threat ended, another would arise, just as it had for their Lord. I have a feeling that some of the young Christians of Thessalonica must have asked, *How long will we have to suffer these kinds of trial and opposition to our faith?*

Paul could not tell them the time their suffering would end, but already in some way the wrath of God was being poured out on some who had opposed the faithful (see 2:16). In time, the final victory would come.

Imitators

The word "imitator" in 1 Thessalonians 2:14 is interesting. In our culture an *imitation* implies a poor attempt to copy something of value. It might be imitation wood on your automobile dash, or imitation seafood in the grocery store. Most of us would avoid an imitation if we could, seeing it as second rate.

Paul had a different idea in mind, however. In Ephesians 5:1, he urged his friends in Christ to "be imitators of God . . . as dearly loved children." He implied the idea of following the highest moral and ethical standards. In the ancient world, the way in which one learned to master the art of oratory was to study and imitate the greatest orators who had gone before. The idea was to learn from and emulate the very best.

Paul's praise of the Thessalonian Christians as "imitators of God's churches" was meant to acknowledge their example, so much in keeping with the intent of God for God's churches. The Thessalonians had demonstrated in their church life the best qualities of God's people.

A Ministry of Opportunity

During seminary days my wife and I were fortunate to serve a rural church not too far from the seminary campus. This small congregation was in a sparsely-settled farming community. Some might consider such a church to be an insignificant church. It was small, with limited facilities, and not a great deal of financial resources. We saw it otherwise. For many years that church has seen a part of its mission as offering seminary students a place for experience and ministry. What words of encouragement and thanks do you think might be appropriate to send to such a congregation?

Questions

1. If a new believer came to you asking you for guidance in how to live out the Christian life, what would you say?

2. Would your suggestions include participation in a church?

3. What qualities exist in your church that would help a new believer to mature in faith?

4. What qualities in your church need to be more effective and helpful in leading a new Christian to maturity?

5. What do you feel to be the greatest challenges to a new believer living in your community?

Focal Text

1 Thessalonians
2:1–12; 5:12–13

Background

1 Thessalonians
2:1–12; 5:12–13

Main Idea

Church leaders inspire followers
when leaders serve God and the
church with faithfulness, integrity,
and love.

LESSON
TEN

Leadership That Inspires Followers

Study Aim

To identify qualities of church leaders who are to be affirmed and followed

Study and Action Emphases

- Affirm the Bible as our authoritative guide for life and ministry
- Share the gospel with all people
- Develop a growing, vibrant faith
- Include all God's family in decision-making and service
- Equip people for servant leadership

Quick Read

Church leaders should learn that shared decision making and integrity of life not only make for good leaders but also encourage others to follow and implement their own faith.

For a number of years my ministry was in the area of church-minister relations for a state Baptist convention. During that time I had the opportunity to work with hundreds of churches looking for ministers and with hundreds more ministers who were open to God's leadership as they sought places of service.

Some of the most inspiring times I enjoyed had to do with visits with young ministers coming out of seminaries and exploring those first places of formal ministry. Often we talked about their understanding of their personality and their style of doing ministry. It was exciting to watch many of them, obviously well-educated and competent, express a devotion to a servant style of ministry in which they were determined to follow the spirit of Christ. I have been able to follow a number of them through the years and see a pattern of excellent service and healthy relationships with their churches. They have often led their congregations through difficult decisions and momentous changes, and they still have found strong support from their churches.

Unfortunately, some saw themselves as leaders whose opinions and ideas were not to be questioned. They were determined to go out to the churches and "straighten out" some of those congregations. Some of these churches probably needed some exhortation. These ministers' autocratic style of leadership, however, inevitably led to conflict, church splits, and forced terminations. Some have left the ministry; others have had numerous conflicts through the years.

Many seemed genuinely puzzled as to why churches did not follow their lead.

What is the difference? In this lesson we will explore some qualities of Christian leadership that inspires others to follow. These qualities of leadership are important for those who serve in all areas of church life, both pulpit and pew.

1 Thessalonians 2:1–12

1You know, brothers, that our visit to you was not a failure. **2**We had previously suffered and been insulted in Philippi, as you know, but with the help of our God we dared to tell you his gospel in spite of strong opposition. **3**For the appeal we make does not spring from error or impure motives, nor are we trying to trick you. **4**On the contrary, we speak as men approved by God to be entrusted with the gospel. We are not trying to please men but God, who tests our hearts. **5**You know we never used flattery, nor did we put on a mask to cover up greed—God is our witness. **6**We were not looking for praise from men, not from you or anyone else.

As apostles of Christ we could have been a burden to you, **7**but we were gentle among you, like a mother caring for her little children. **8**We loved you so much that we were delighted to share with you not only the gospel of God but our lives as well, because you had become so dear to us. **9**Surely you remember, brothers, our toil and hardship; we worked night and day in order not to be a burden to anyone while we preached the gospel of God to you.

10You are witnesses, and so is God, of how holy, righteous and blameless we were among you who believed. **11**For you know that we dealt with each of you as a father deals with his own children, **12**encouraging, comforting and urging you to live lives worthy of God, who calls you into his kingdom and glory.

1 Thessalonians 5:12–13

12Now we ask you, brothers, to respect those who work hard among you, who are over you in the Lord and who admonish you. **13**Hold them in the highest regard in love because of their work. Live in peace with each other.

A Team Approach to Ministry (2:1)

Both Thessalonian letters begin in the same way, identifying them as coming from "Paul, Silas and Timothy" (1 Thessalonians 1:1; 2 Thessalonians 1:1). From the beginning Paul shared his missionary task. Names like Barnabas, Mark, Silas, Timothy, and others appear in Acts as Paul's missionary journeys unfolded. Luke, usually considered to be the author of Acts, also seems to have been there recording important events. Men and women joined forces with Paul and his companions to establish churches and spread the gospel. These names make it clear that Paul's was no lone ministry. The task was much larger than one person could attempt alone.

Although Paul is usually considered to be the author of these letters, it is not hard to imagine that the three leaders—"Paul, Silas and Timothy"—sat together and discussed the content. Throughout 1 and 2 Thessalonians, the use of the pronoun "we" indicates that this is a collaborative message. The group had gone to Thessalonica together in the beginning of their ministry there. Forced to leave because of the misunderstanding and opposition of some, they longed to know how the new church fared. So Timothy had been sent back for continuing contact. His report inspired these letters of praise and thanksgiving to God and to the faithful saints in the church at Thessalonica.

Men and women joined forces with Paul and his companions to establish churches and spread the gospel.

Why a team approach? Teams offer continuing help for leaders in sharing insight and approaches to ministry. Teams help to avoid the love of power and position and an absence of accountability that seems to afflict so many who demand absolute control of leadership roles. As Paul prepared for his second missionary journey, a dispute arose between Paul and Barnabas about the wisdom of taking John Mark with them. Shared leadership wisely ended up with a win/win solution. Paul would take Silas, and Barnabas would take Mark. As a result, in spite of the dispute, two teams were at work (Acts 15:36–40).

If the priesthood of all believers is to be lived out in the life of the church, there must be a shared leadership rather than dictatorial leaders who demand unquestioned loyalty.

A precious insight of Scripture that has helped shape our Baptist heritage is the reality of the priesthood of all believers. Not only does this mean that we all have free access to God's grace and presence without human intermediaries, but it also means that we have responsibilities for involvement in ministry. If the priesthood of all believers is to be lived out in the life of the church, there must be a shared leadership rather than dictatorial leaders who demand unquestioned loyalty.

The Spirit of Christian Leadership (2:1–6a)

These brief verses tell us much about the spirit of the missionary team as they came to Thessalonica. Through the tone of the writing and the compassion of their words, we learn much about their motives and attitudes as they went about their work of the gospel.

First, the courage and determination of Paul and his group in coming to Thessalonica in the beginning demonstrated much about their leadership. On more than one occasion Paul and the others had boldly shared their faith, only to be met by determined detractors, angry mobs, or the ridicule of some who claimed to be wise (see Acts 13:8–10, 49–50; 14:2–5, 19–20; 16:19–24). Many would take these difficult responses as reason enough to abandon the mission. Paul and his companions, though, would not be stopped by the resistance of unbelievers. As one door closed they moved on to a new location to share the gospel.

Second, it is worth noting that they did not come using techniques that could be described as manipulative (see especially 1 Thess. 2:3). They instead came as confident witnesses, relying on the truth they had come to experience in a personal relationship with their Lord.

We should be reminded of the temptation experience in which Jesus was tempted to use spectacular methods to draw crowds and he would not (Matthew 4:5–7). Even the miracle events at the hands of Jesus were not attempts to persuade people by mere spectacles. Instead, each pointed to some great truth by which Jesus sought to draw people to God's grace.

True leaders make clear their desire to see those they lead succeed in the important things of life.

Third, note that Paul, Silas, and Timothy had not served in ways so as to seek popular approval or praise from the people. More than anything else, they came seeking to be true to the message of Christ and Christ's love that had so changed their lives. Truly they came with great reverence for the truth of salvation through Christ alone.

The Qualities of Christian Leaders (2:6b–12)

Outlined in these verses are several qualities of Christian leadership that were demonstrated in the lives and words of Paul and his missionary associates. As you read these verses, look for the appealing images, emotions, and insights that are mentioned as the team poured out a message of encouragement.

What a blessing it must have been to the young Christians to know their mentors were praying for them, encouraging them, and believing in their possibilities.

We see an obvious compassionate concern for the new believers. One cannot miss the spirit of caring that characterizes both 1 and 2 Thessalonians. Although there were issues that needed to be emphasized with firmness, we do not see harsh or judgmental words or attitudes. Listen to the reminder, "We were gentle among you, like a mother caring for her little children" (2:7).

Note the manner of their leadership (2:8). They did not come as aloof teachers or unapproachable authorities but as those who not only shared a message but life experiences. Working alongside them, the new believers must have learned from the example of the more experienced visitors in dealing with daily experiences as well as from their preaching or teaching.

Most of us can remember a teacher, a pastor, or a business executive whose open door policy meant much to us. We not only benefited from their official pronouncements but even more from the informal times when these people made us feel our concerns were important. Together we sought answers to questions or problems. Observing how they lived became important learning experiences.

Too, the traveling missionaries worked hard to avoid being a burden to the young church (2:9). Acts 18:3 tells us that Paul could support himself through his skill as a tentmaker. Perhaps he and the others worked at some such trade to support themselves while carrying on their preaching mission.

Authority in leadership does not result from position or title.

In 2 Thessalonians 3:7–8, Paul would again mention this matter of work to support his contention that everyone should avoid idleness. That emphasis will be the focus of another lesson in this series.

Another quality that emerged from the careful and thoughtful manner of their ministry was an obvious integrity in their efforts (1 Thess. 2:10). The first-century world was filled with traveling pseudo-prophets, magicians, and scam artists. Their skill with words and persuasion brought them fame and fortune, but in the end their methods were empty charades. There must have been a strong sense of suspicion and doubt surrounding any itinerant philosopher or religious speaker who came to town. The preaching team brought by Paul would have to prove itself worthy of being taken seriously. In 2 Corinthians 2:17 Paul shared a basic philosophy that demonstrated his sensitivity in financial matters. He wrote, "Unlike so many, we do not peddle the word of God for profit." On the other hand, in his appeal to the Thessalonian believers he would invite their observation of "how holy, and righteous and blameless" had been the manner of the team's work among them (1 Thess. 2:10).

Leaders attain authority in the eyes of congregations by their example of devotion, hard work, and obvious commitment to Christ and Christ's people.

An additional and very obvious quality of the team's leadership was their patient and persistent teaching (2:11–12). Their patience showed in that they gently but firmly encouraged, inspired, and challenged their young friends in Christ. Indeed, throughout the letter we see many ways in which Paul and his associates labored tirelessly to see that the emerging church in Thessalonica could have access to the truth of Christ.

Finally, we cannot fail to see throughout these two letters a continuing concern for this congregation. Even though Paul and his associates had to make a hasty and unscheduled departure, they maintained a deep concern to help these new believers grow and mature. Indeed they were even more determined in their absence to follow up on the progress and the needs of the church they had helped to plant.

True leaders make clear their desire to see those they lead succeed in the important things of life. A glimpse at 1 Thessalonians 3:11–13 shows a prayer the team made for the church. The prayer reveals a longing to return and renew their friendship in Christ and to continue the joyous relationship begun on their first visit. What a blessing it must have been to the young Christians to know their mentors were praying for them, encouraging them, and believing in their possibilities.

These several qualities of leadership are admirable and timeless. They are qualities that can be useful by those who serve in positions throughout the life of the church, in pulpit and pew alike.

An Authority Earned Through Example (5:12–13)

The missionary team challenged the Thessalonian church to give respect and support to its leaders. This support would emerge as the people observed their leaders and sensed their commitment and sincerity.

Authority in leadership does not result from position or title. We live in an age that is increasingly skeptical of the claims of Christ. No longer is the message of preacher, teacher, and church leader simply taken as fact because of its coming from the church. It will be increasingly necessary for church leaders to demonstrate strong and credible leadership qualities, sensitive to the ideas and insights and experiences of all. A very wise teacher used to tell his classes of young ministers, "In the New Testament there are no offices to be filled; there are services to be rendered." Leaders see the needs of a world around them and seek to mobilize others out of a genuine concern.

The prayer of every leader must be that he or she be so filled with the spirit of Christ that Christ's mission is extended to the world around us.

The authority of a leader is not something that can be demanded. Leaders attain authority in the eyes of congregations by their example of devotion, hard work, and obvious commitment to Christ and Christ's people. Our authority in ministry comes from the calling of God himself, but we serve in a community of people who must observe that the leader truly cares for them. When that is obvious, people will follow.

Our example in leadership is most firmly rooted in Jesus. He has continued to draw people to salvation because history has seen no greater example of sacrificial devotion to his purpose and to the people he came to serve. He earned the respect of those who saw what he was truly about. As they observed Jesus at work in the towns and villages, in homes and fishing camps, in marketplaces and temple courts, they saw one who lived out the truth of God's love and grace.

There is no greater privilege than to be asked to serve in some leadership role in our church. It is to be hoped that the invitation has come because someone has observed gifts of leadership that can help the church fulfill its mission. Leadership, however, is more than being a name on the Nominating Committee's report, elected by the church at its business meeting. Leadership has to do with helping the church accomplish its purposes with the maximum involvement of others in the process.

The prayer of every leader must be that he or she be so filled with the spirit of Christ that Christ's mission is extended to the world around us. Such leadership inspires others to become involved in kingdom work.

Courageous Leadership

The small town of Urbanna, Virginia, was the scene of one of the more dramatic moments in Baptist history in the United States. In colonial times in Virginia, John Waller, a pioneer Baptist pastor, was brought before a judge and charged with preaching without a license from the established church in the colony. Waller and his fellow preachers were given a choice to cease preaching or go to jail.

With great courage, Waller insisted that no Baptist minister should choose freedom at the expense of conscience. In a cold Virginia winter they were jailed for their convictions on freedom of conscience.

An interesting note is that the foundation of the Urbanna Baptist Church is built of bricks from the jail where Waller was imprisoned. His courage outlasted the opposition of an established church. Needless to say, the Baptists of that area are often inspired by remembering the suffering of an early generation of Baptist leaders.

Examining our Leadership

Paul and his companions in ministry demonstrated several leadership characteristics that can serve as guidance for our leadership efforts. How evident are these in your life and in the leaders you follow?

- They spoke truth of which they were confident.

- The motive in their ministry was compassion.

- They did not seek to deceive people or trick them into joining something they did not fully believe.

- They spoke, not to please crowds of people, but to be true to God's revelation of himself in Christ.

- They had no interest in financial gain.

- They would let the results speak for themselves rather than seeking praise.

Questions

1. How do you feel about a team concept of leadership such as is implied in 1 Thessalonians 1:1? Have you experienced team leadership in the setting of a church?

2. Have there been times when you have faced criticism that tempted you to silence your witness or compromise your convictions? What helped you in those circumstances?

3. Think of leaders who have most influenced your life as a Christian through the years. What were the qualities in their leadership that made them effective? How evident are these qualities in leaders in your church? in you?

4. What are some ways that you or your church could show appreciation and support for those who serve in leadership roles in the church?

Focal Text

1 Thessalonians
4:1–12; 5:14–22

Background

1 Thessalonians
4:1–12; 5:14–22

Main Idea

Christians are to live so as to please
God and bless others.

Question to Explore

What's distinctive about the
Christian lifestyle?

LESSON ELEVEN

Instructions for Lives That Please God

Study Aim

To measure myself by qualities of life that please God and bless others

Study and Action Emphases

- Affirm the Bible as our authoritative guide for life and ministry
- Share the gospel with all people
- Develop a growing, vibrant faith
- Encourage healthy families
- Obey and serve Jesus by meeting physical, spiritual, and emotional needs
- Equip people for servant leadership

Quick Read

While salvation is a gift of God's grace, those who receive this blessing have an obligation to live out their faith in every aspect of daily living. We do this, not to earn God's favor but to express God's love through our lives that others may know his salvation.

Sitting at a table one Wednesday evening as I waited to speak to a stewardship emphasis, I chatted with the fellow on my left. I casually inquired about his employment. He proceeded to tell me about his business, which he went on to say was a trade in a product most church people frowned on. He hastened to say, "What I do on Monday has nothing to do with what I do for my church." Unfortunately his attitude is echoed by too many in our churches today. It is not so much their product, but the idea that their relationship with Christ has little or nothing to do with the influence and example of their lives throughout the week.

Very early in the history of Christianity a problem arose. There were those who felt that if one is saved by the grace of God, not on a basis of merit or having earned it, then why not keep on living sinful lives so God could have the privilege of forgiving us even more! Goodness could wait for a heavenly existence while an unbridled life unfolded in this earthly life.

You may remember the way Paul put this issue when he wrote to the Romans (Romans 6:1): "Shall we go on sinning so that grace may increase? By no means! We died to sin; how can we live in it any longer?" Paul recognized that not only was immoral behavior a denial of true faith, but also that it would do great violence to the credibility of Christian witness. God expected more of his people.

In the little epistle of Jude is another reminder of this truth. "For certain men . . . have secretly slipped in among you. They are godless men, who change the grace of our God into a license for immorality and deny Jesus Christ our only Sovereign and Lord" (Jude 4). From early days, some have wanted to presume on the grace of God as an excuse for careless living.

Being a Christian is much more than just "being good," but an upright and disciplined life is an essential part of an obedient life. Just what does God expect in the lives of people who claim Christ as Lord? Every culture and religion has its codes of behavior that are seen as desirable. What is there in the example of Jesus and the transforming power of the Holy Spirit that is central to a Christian lifestyle?

1 Thessalonians 4:1–12

1Finally, brothers, we instructed you how to live in order to please God, as in fact you are living. Now we ask you and urge you in the Lord Jesus to do this more and more. **2**For you know what instructions we gave you by the authority of the Lord Jesus.

3It is God's will that you should be sanctified: that you should avoid sexual immorality; **4**that each of you should learn to control his own body in a way that is holy and honorable, **5**not in passionate lust like the heathen, who do not know God; **6**and that in this matter no one should wrong his brother or take advantage of him. The Lord will punish men for all such sins, as we have already told you and warned you. **7**For God did not call us to be impure, but to live a holy life. **8**Therefore, he who rejects this instruction does not reject man but God, who gives you his Holy Spirit.

9Now about brotherly love we do not need to write to you, for you yourselves have been taught by God to love each other. **10**And in fact, you do love all the brothers throughout Macedonia. Yet we urge you, brothers, to do so more and more.

11Make it your ambition to lead a quiet life, to mind your own business and to work with your hands, just as we told you, **12**so that your daily life may win the respect of outsiders and so that you will not be dependent on anybody.

1 Thessalonians 5:14–22

14And we urge you, brothers, warn those who are idle, encourage the timid, help the weak, be patient with everyone. **15**Make sure that nobody pays back wrong for wrong, but always try to be kind to each other and to everyone else.

16Be joyful always; **17**pray continually; **18**give thanks in all circumstances, for this is God's will for you in Christ Jesus.

19Do not put out the Spirit's fire; **20**do not treat prophecies with contempt. **21**Test everything. Hold on to the good. **22**Avoid every kind of evil.

A Reminder of Earlier Instruction (4:1–2)

Paul and his team were aware from their first contacts in Thessalonica of the necessity of instruction for those coming from a culture shaped by vastly different values from those of the way of Christ. In these first verses of chapter 4 he reminded them of what must have been intensive instruction while the team was there. It was instruction in "how to live in order to please God" (4:1). An

> *"What I do on Monday has nothing to do with what I do for my church."*

important part of the work that the missionaries had done was to nurture new believers through instruction in godly living.

The Christian faith was known from its earliest days as "the Way" (see Acts 9:1-2). The Christian faith is not merely doctrines or speculations on the future. It is a way of life that must reflect the nature and purpose of God in human life. In the memorable words from the Sermon on the Mount (Matthew 5—7), Jesus taught, "Let your light shine before others, so that they may see your good works and give glory to your Father in heaven" (Matthew 5:16, NRSV). Believers' most impressive witness would occur through example and the demonstration of changed lives.

The instructions Paul and his associates gave to the Thessalonians had "the authority of the Lord Jesus" (1 Thess. 4:2). They were not based on speculation or arbitrary restrictions, and neither were they an opinion by the teachers. They were instructions that were theologically grounded in the will of God for God's people. These instructions grew out of Paul's understanding of who God is and what God is doing in this world.

The Principle of Holiness (4:3a)

Verse 3 begins with a statement that sets the stage for all that follows. "It is God's will that you should be sanctified." The instruction that had been given to the faithful in Thessalonica was nothing less than the will of God for God's people. Again, these were not merely religious rules or the opinions of church leaders. This state of holiness was in progress in the lives of these Christians, and they must press on toward the goal of obedience.

From early days, some have wanted to presume on the grace of God as an excuse for careless living.

Unfortunately the idea of holiness, if not entirely absent from our vocabulary, has taken a negative note in our time. We tend to think of holiness, or its related concept of sanctification, as merely refraining from various behaviors. In Scripture this word is a beautifully descriptive word, reflecting the concept of the nature and character of God being lived out in human beings (see Leviticus 11:44, NRSV).

A Specific Application (4:3b–8)

In beginning this set of instructions for the godly life, Paul moved directly to the issue of sexual conduct. This is certainly not the only area of holy living, but it receives considerable attention in this section, for good cause in light of the situation in Thessalonica.

The culture out of which the Thessalonian Christians emerged presented a totally different set of moral standards and behavioral practices than those of a Christian perspective. No doubt Paul and his companions stressed a nobler understanding of human sexuality in leading the young believers to understand God's intentions.

Just what does God expect in the lives of people who claim Christ as Lord?

In the Roman Empire, a man would have a wife to bear children, and he felt some obligation to support the wife's needs. It was quite common in that day, however, for a man to engage in a variety of extramarital liaisons as he might choose. Christian men were to show a nobler respect for women and for sexual expression. Christians were not to be like the "heathen, who do not know God" (4:5).

Even among Jews of the first century who held the idea of marriage as important, divorce had become quite common and was easily obtained. We need only look at our own culture to see how we have weakened the concept of commitment between those entering marriage. We have strict legal requirements for licenses for marriage, and we go to great lengths in public ceremonies of marriage. A license and a ceremony, however, do not make a marriage! The commitment of a man and a woman to love, honor, and cherish each other, under the authority of God, forms the setting for a true marriage. That kind of relationship is the appropriate place for sexual relations.

The commitment of a man and a woman to love, honor, and cherish each other, under the authority of God, forms the setting for a true marriage.

In the biblical view, sexual relations are intended to be the expression of a committed love within a monogamous relationship. Far from being simply a recreational activity for the pleasure of a person, sexual intercourse for the Christian must be seen in the context of the total Christian life. As such, the emphasis is as much on giving as receiving.

The expression of sexuality has implications for those who are married and also for those who are dating, working in the presence of other people, or simply engaging in social interaction in which the stimulation of sexual interest can occur. In all instances, the guiding principle is being "holy and honorable" (4:3).

One must take seriously the impact of such actions on one's individual life, the life of one's spouse or friend, and the lives of other people who are directly affected by that behavior. We all know people who have hurt others grievously by inappropriate sexual behavior. Even in marriage, sexual relationships can be abusive and miss the mark of holy and honorable behavior.

Again, verse 8 reminds us that there is a divine mandate to these words. They are not just pastoral advice. They are words and concepts that carry the authority of God. To be sure, voices in the Gentile world appealed for sexual purity lest the individual be disgraced. Paul's appeal, however, was based on the authority of God, to whom we must ultimately answer.

The Principle of Love As the Foundation of Godly Living (4:9–10)

"Brotherly love" includes all the "brothers and sisters," as the New Revised Standard Version reminds us (4:9). Paul was speaking here about the relationship of believers. All of God's people are to be treated on the basis of a loving relationship. Just as they have been "loved by God" (1:4), so they are to love one another.

In this matter Paul commended the Thessalonian Christians for their example of love within the household of faith. How different from the stern admonition he directed at the Corinthian church, which fell short of this great example (1 Corinthians 1:10–12).

One could ask how he could say they love "all the brothers throughout Macedonia" (4:10). What contact could the Thessalonians have had or how could they have known all those people? To grasp his meaning we must understand the nature of *agape* love. Such love is not sentimentality or personal affection. *Agape* is an active work for the good of others. It could involve prayer, financial support, or hospitality for others. Indeed, Paul's collection for the saints in Jerusalem would take special root in Macedonia. In these and other ways the Thessalonian Christians had demonstrated an exemplary love toward the larger Christian fellowship. For this Paul commended them.

The Winsome Life (4:11–12)

Just what the text means by a "quiet life" is not entirely clear. It likely has to do with a life that does not create a disturbance or unnecessarily call attention to itself. In some secular writings of that day, living "quietly" is contrasted with being a busybody who noses into the affairs of others. Those Christians who lived out their faith in an often hostile setting would suffer often for their convictions. They should not, however, provoke trouble. Someone once said that anyone can get crucified in this life. For a Christian, it should be over something redemptive!

"Mind your own business and . . . work with your hands" is Paul's way of reminding his young Christian friends of one of the most important ways in which they would live respectable lives (4:12). It would be through the kind of life that was pleasing to God. Why? "So that your daily life may win the respect of outsiders and so that you will not be dependent on anybody" (4:12). We must not read into this any suggestion that they be unconcerned about the needs of others. This would be quite unlike the love of which Paul had just spoken. Paul may have simply had in mind a faith community whose winsome lifestyle showed a quality that would draw others to faith.

A Summary of a Worthy Life (5:14–22)

We come to this final section to deal with a question of how Christians in the church are to treat those who are struggling and losing heart. The reality of the times and the lack of mature faith would no doubt mean some would begin to pull away from faithfulness. We can imagine a picture of those who had grown weary with the Christian way. They were undisciplined and inactive. How should those who wished to live godly lives treat those they considered weak in their commitment?

Basically, the life that is pleasing to God is a life lived with reverence, respect, and a sense of purpose, all rooted in a relationship with God.

Paul mentioned responses to some specific situations with simple advice. For those who are "idle" ("unruly" in the NASB), those who are "timid," and those who are "weak" (5:14), Paul's advice was to "warn," "encourage," and "help." In a nutshell, help them, don't shun them. Paul would sometime later write to the Romans a more detailed exhortation about dealing with strengths and weaknesses in individuals in the church (Romans 14:1–15).

We would do well to heed these words in an age when many churches are perceived as seeking to exclude all those who are different or whose lives fail to measure up to some assumed checklist of moral regulations. The New Testament record of the behavior of the Pharisees, with their strict and unyielding insistence on adherence to a code of religious rules, shows the danger of such an approach. Jesus, on the other hand, was known for his acceptance and inclusion of so many of those whom organized religion had excluded.

Jesus . . . was known for his acceptance and inclusion of so many of those whom organized religion had excluded.

Kindness (1 Thess. 5:15) may well be the operative word in this approach to the strugglers in the church. Kindness seems to be the lost virtue in too much contemporary religion. We are clear on issues of right and wrong, but we are so harsh in the treatment of those who fail. We are busy in acts of service and benevolence, but so much good is lost by an unkind and haughty spirit.

The last verses of our text (5:16–22) seem to sing with a spirit of a life rooted and grounded in a faith relationship with Christ. There is a joy that transcends the difficult circumstances of life. There is a prayer of thanksgiving on the lips of the faithful, no matter how tough the circumstances, because Christ has lifted the vision of the believer to a higher calling. The Spirit of God is the source of strength and discernment that enables believers to take a courageous stance in the face of all that life hurls at us.

Basically, the life that is pleasing to God is a life lived with reverence, respect, and a sense of purpose, all rooted in a relationship with God. Such a life is much more than one in which certain sins are carefully avoided. There must be a positive expression in the godly life of God's love in action toward others. Such a life must be lived out daily, and it must be reflective of the way of Jesus, our perfect example.

Saints

The term *saint* comes from the word that means *holy* and is applied in the New Testament to all believers in Jesus as the Christ. To be a saint is not a matter of being inhuman or withdrawing from the world. Rather, being a saint has to do with godliness in this world, living a life pleasing to God in the realm of the most basic and intimate human relationships.

The saint lives for God's purposes. Early in Christian history, the church especially revered those witnesses who were martyred for their faith, according them special recognition as saints. Later the term was applied only to a few select people who had done significant service. Limiting the application of the term *saint* is to miss a meaningful New Testament insight that all believers are set apart for holy living and service.

Choosing the Christian Way

Living the Christian life requires a partnership with God. Jesus' example and the Holy Spirit's creative power are linked with human beings who must decide their manner of living each day. Consider these questions as you decide your lifestyle choices:

- Does this action reflect the example of Jesus?

- Will this action help or hurt another person?

- Is this action done from an unselfish motive?

- Will the kingdom of God be enhanced if I take this course of action?

Questions

1. One of Paul's great affirmations is that salvation comes through the grace of God, not by religious works (see Ephesians 2:8–9). If salvation is by grace, why is it important for a Christian to produce good works in his or her life?

2. What are some issues of our modern culture that call for a Christian response and a different lifestyle? What applications of the Scriptures of this lesson can you see to these issues?

3. The primary mission of the church must be to represent the love of God in this world so that others may come to know God's saving grace. How can we live out our faith with integrity and not create the impression that people without a personal relationship with Christ are unwelcome in our midst?

4. In what ways does your church offer ministries that encourage and strengthen struggling people? Are there other things your church might do to reach selected groups in your community?

Focal Text

1 Thessalonians
4:13—5:11

Background

1 Thessalonians
4:13—5:11;
2 Thessalonians
1:5—2:12

Main Idea

Christ's resurrection and promised
return provide assurance that we
and our loved ones who trust in
Christ are with Christ, in death as
well as in life.

Question to Explore

What hope is there
when death comes?

LESSON TWELVE

Hope for Loved Ones and Ourselves

Study Aim

To recognize the hope Christ offers me and my loved ones when death comes

Study and Action Emphases

- Affirm the Bible as our authoritative guide for life and ministry
- Share the gospel with all people
- Develop a growing, vibrant faith
- Obey and serve Jesus by meeting physical, spiritual, and emotional needs

Quick Read

While grief is the natural response to loss, faith in the risen Christ can provide hope that delivers believers from despair in the face of death.

The accident was one of the most tragic I had ever had to deal with. A wonderful couple from our church, along with their teen-aged son, had left our city very early one morning to beat the morning rush hour traffic on their way to visit their daughter who lived a couple of states away. Some thirty miles out of our city, they rounded a curve and were hit head on by a drunk driver who was on the wrong side of the highway. All of them were killed instantly.

I went with a friend later that day to the airport to meet the daughter and another son as they arrived to make arrangements for their parents' funeral. We left the airport, my friend and I in silence as brother and sister talked in shocked voices of the tragedy. There are no words to take away such grief. In a flash they had lost their parents and younger brother. Places in their lives would forever be empty. The pain of the loss was overpowering.

Finally, my friend and I heard the brother say to his sister, "At least we know they were saved. We don't have to worry about that." The reality of a saving relationship with Christ was the most comforting thought they could bring to mind. It would be their source of hope and comfort for years to come as they dealt with the lingering reality of their loss.

One reality of life is that death comes to all of us and it touches those around us, leaving its inevitable trail of pain and sorrow. Imagine not having a hope to give courage and consolation!

1 Thessalonians 4:13–18

13Brothers, we do not want you to be ignorant about those who fall asleep, or to grieve like the rest of men, who have no hope. **14**We believe that Jesus died and rose again and so we believe that God will bring with Jesus those who have fallen asleep in him. **15**According to the Lord's own word, we tell you that we who are still alive, who are left till the coming of the Lord, will certainly not precede those who have fallen asleep. **16**For the Lord himself will come down from heaven, with a loud command, with the voice of the archangel and with the trumpet call of God, and the dead in Christ will rise first. **17**After that, we who are still alive and are left will be caught up together with them in the clouds to meet the Lord in the air. And so we will be with the Lord forever. **18**Therefore encourage each other with these words.

1 Thessalonians 5:1–11

1Now, brothers, about times and dates we do not need to write to you, **2**for you know very well that the day of the Lord will come like a thief in the night. **3**While people are saying, "Peace and safety," destruction will come on them suddenly, as labor pains on a pregnant woman, and they will not escape.

4But you, brothers, are not in darkness so that this day should surprise you like a thief. **5**You are all sons of the light and sons of the day. We do not belong to the night or to the darkness. **6**So then, let us not be like others, who are asleep, but let us be alert and self-controlled. **7**For those who sleep, sleep at night, and those who get drunk, get drunk at night. **8**But since we belong to the day, let us be self-controlled, putting on faith and love as a breastplate, and the hope of salvation as a helmet. **9**For God did not appoint us to suffer wrath but to receive salvation through our Lord Jesus Christ. **10**He died for us so that, whether we are awake or asleep, we may live together with him. **11**Therefore encourage one another and build each other up, just as in fact you are doing.

Grief, the Normal Response to Loss

As a pastor working with grieving people, I have often heard them express guilt and shame over their expression of grief at the loss of loved ones. I have said to many of them that tears are God's gift to express emotions when words won't come. Grieving people do not need to apologize for tears over their loss. In that memorable verse from John 11:35, "Jesus wept." Whether it was for the loss of his friend, his sympathy for Mary and Martha, or his sorrow that they had not yet understood the truth of eternal life, that statement about Jesus remains a testimony of Scripture that Jesus was not immune to tears.

Grief is a normal response to loss, but for a Christian whose loved one has put his or her eternal destiny in God's hands, there is a new way of seeing death. We are not left with only an empty place in our hearts, and neither are we confronted with a God who is oblivious to our feelings. The gospel of Christ is built on Christ's experiences of life, death, and resurrection, realities that transform the way we face what is often called the final enemy—death.

Grief and Hope (4:13–18)

There was a strong belief in the church that the Lord would return soon and usher in the climactic Day of the Lord. Reflected throughout this letter are references to Paul's convictions on the matter, so deeply held that he must have stressed them in his earlier visit. Chapter 1 opens

> *Grief is a normal response to loss. . . .*

with thanks for their "endurance inspired by hope in our Lord Jesus Christ" (1:3). Paul rejoiced in the witness to their reputation as those who "wait for his Son from heaven" (1:10). Paul's prayer in 3:13 is that they will be "blameless and holy in the presence of our God and Father when our Lord Jesus comes with all his holy ones."

At the time of the writing of 1 Thessalonians, some of the Christians of Thessalonica were concerned

189

about Christians who died before the return of Christ. How would they relate to the risen Lord and to those who remained alive at his appearing? Would they somehow not enjoy the same blessings as those who were there at Christ's coming, or would they miss something? One can imagine the Thessalonian Christians' concern, coming as they did from a cultural and religious background that had little in the way of hope beyond the grave.

One reality of life is that death comes to all of us and it touches those around us, leaving its inevitable trail of pain and sorrow.

Nothing in the text tells us what might have prompted their anxiety. Paul's use of the term "asleep" is felt by most scholars to be a clear reference to death. In all likelihood there had been deaths in the congregation. That small band of believers, so much in need of one another, would all have shared the grief. Perhaps their questions also had to do with their wondering what might happen to them should they die before the Lord's return.

We are not told how Paul and his missionary companions learned of their concerns. It may well have been reported to them by Timothy on his return from the visit mentioned in 3:2 as he brought his report on their progress in the faith. Along with the good news he brought of their faithfulness and vitality, he likely shared this concern that troubled some.

At any rate, Paul moved to the heart of the matter in these verses, introduced with the compassionate statement, "We do not want you to be ignorant . . . " (4:13a). This expression does not imply a lack of intellect on the part of his friends. The expression is used as Paul's way of saying that he did not want them uninformed about serious issues. Because the missionary team cared deeply for these people, Paul and his associates would not want to leave them struggling with an issue that had apparently caused deep distress and discussion.

Paul's prayer was not that they would feel no grief at the death of friends and loved ones. Instead, his challenge was that their grief would be framed in the reality of their Lord's death and resurrection (4:14). The secular philosophers of that day urged people not to be overcome by grief through simply accepting death as a part of life. They urged reason as the source of help. On the other hand, Paul and his companions found in the truth of Christ's resurrection the basis of their hope. Jesus' resurrection was an evidence of the love and power of God that reaches beyond death to everlasting life.

Jesus' resurrection was an evidence of the love and power of God that reaches beyond death to everlasting life.

Paul then gave a dramatic picture of the last days in obvious apocalyptic language. Rather than spending time in trying to identify the "loud command," the "trumpet call," and the ascending and descending in the sky of this drama, look at the larger impact of these words. Something spectacular happens that implies power and majesty. The importance of these words is not as a literal description of the last days but rather as a witness to the victory of Christ. There is a drawing together of all the saints, living and dead, into the presence of Christ. Too, there is no advantage or disadvantage to those who have died before this special day.

As tempting as it is to try to identify events as current evidence of the impending appearing of Christ, history tells us we do so with great peril.

With these insights, the believers are challenged to "encourage each other with these words" (4:18). Rather than finding hope in human reason and self-control, they were to find their hope in the fact of the final victory of history that lies in the power of the Lord who defeats the enemy "with the breath of his mouth" (2 Thessalonians 2:8). Such language is intended to contrast the power of the risen Lord with the limitations of all who oppose or reject him.

Tell Us When (5:1–3)

From earliest times minds have pondered the timing of the return of Christ. In the text before us we learn that a feeling had arisen among some of the Thessalonians that the Day of the Lord had already occurred. Could this be? The background passage in 2 Thessalonians 1:5—2:12 makes clear that this is not the case. The long anticipated Day will come only in God's timing, revealing God's power and majesty and the impotence of all who resist him. There are chapters of history and personalities that must yet unfold.

As tempting as it is to try to identify events as current evidence of the impending appearing of Christ, history tells us we do so with great peril. For instance, in 2 Thessalonians Paul speaks of the "man of lawlessness" (2:3) who must come before the Day of the Lord. While not calling this person "antichrist," the role seems appropriate (see 1 John 2:18, 22). Historically, hundreds of people have been identified as this resister of Christ. There have been those who identified the Antichrist as the Pope on one hand, and Luther on the other. In our own day this mysterious one has been variously identified as Hitler, Stalin, Gorbachev, Saddam Hussein, Osama bin Laden, as well as assorted other kings, presidents, and world figures. The outbreak of the Gulf War in 1990–91 brought scores of would-be prophets to their pulpits with specific messages stating emphatically that this was the biblical Armageddon that would herald the coming of Christ.

However and whenever it comes, the Day of the Lord will come as "a thief in the night" (1 Thess. 5:2), not with billboards announcing the date and time. We live in a world with the presence of evil that warrants the wrath of God. Who or what is holding back that wrath remains in God's knowledge (2 Thess. 2:7). The final and ultimate expression of judgment is in the hands of the Almighty. God alone knows the schedule.

There will always be mystery here. These words come from the Apostle who would later have to say, "Now we see but a poor reflection as in a mirror; then we shall see face to face. Now I know in part; then I shall know fully, even as I am fully known" (1 Corinthians 13:12). Again, he would say to the Corinthians, "We live by faith, not by sight" (2 Corinthians 5:7). The Johannine epistle reminds us again: "Dear friends, now we are children of God, and what we will be has not yet been made known. But we know that when he appears, we shall be like him, for we will see him as he is. Everyone who has this hope in him purifies himself, just as he is pure" (1 John 3:2–3).

Paul and his associates did not intend to tell us or the Thessalonians when or exactly how all this would occur. It was enough for Paul to call his friends in Christ to be confident about the future and to live out the love of God in every aspect of their lives in the here and now.

In the Meantime (5:4–11)

This passage may well contain the heart of the matter as we deal with the question of the return of the Lord. Since the timing is a mystery, readiness is the key word. Paul's challenge, "So then, let us not be like others, who are asleep, but let us be alert and self-controlled" (5:6). His use of the term "asleep" here obviously is not a reference to death, but rather to the kind of careless attitude that characterized some people. The Christian must use this lifetime as a preparation for the Day of the Lord. The Christian emphasis is on *eternal* life, for which we are already preparing.

Christians are not in "the darkness" about these things. They live in the light of God's truth and have ample warning in that truth. The appeal is for them to live in sobriety, which may refer to a life of calm and controlled readiness. The Greek verb in the phrase, "let us be self-controlled," is in the present tense, which means it is an ongoing action.

Paul and his associates did not intend to tell us or the Thessalonians when or exactly how all this would occur.

In living out this spirit of readiness, Paul called on three great virtues to guide the Thessalonian Christians' lives. They are "faith," "love," and "hope" (5:8). These virtues are the ingredients of a life that is lived in readiness. They are active words, implying a confident trust in God's control and an active involvement in living out the implications in this world. Behind this kind of living is the sure knowledge of God's salvation that will be fulfilled in due time. The Thessalonian Christians' task now was faithfulness and readiness.

Paul did not answer here what may have been another question in the minds of his friends, as well as ours. *What is the nature of our existence after death and before the Day of the Lord?* Elsewhere we read some insights into the mystery of our eternal existence. In 1 Corinthians 15:51 we are told that "We will not all sleep, but we will all be changed," and in 2 Corinthians 5:6–10 and Philippians 1:23 we read that in death we will be with Christ. Paul left the details of the mystery unexplained.

The importance of Christian faith in the face of death lies not in having all the answers to the details of our future existence or in having an explanation of tragedy, illness, and loss. The importance of Christian faith in dealing with such questions lies, rather, in confident faith and abiding trust

> *The Christian must use this lifetime as a preparation for the Day of the Lord.*

in the God who has worked for our redemption, who walks with us through the valleys and shadows of day-to-day existence, and who will be there in the future to receive us into his presence beyond the grave. "Therefore, encourage each other with these words" (1 Thess. 4:18).

Day of the Lord

The Old Testament prophets saw a day of reckoning on the horizon, a day in which the proud and arrogant would come face to face with the majesty and power of God. While many pious folk spoke with great anticipation of the coming Day of the Lord, Amos warned that it would be a day of frightening accountability. It would be accompanied with inescapable judgment, of darkness and not light (Amos 5:18–20).

The New Testament adds another element to the idea of the Day of the Lord, tied closely with the *parousia*, or coming, of the Lord. The gospel brings the element of the final redemption of the faithful (Ephesians 4:30). Among the faithful, it is a time of encouragement and fulfillment rather than a situation eliciting fear. As such it is an occasion to glorify and praise the Lord.

A Case Study on Hope

A young woman told a student conference the tragic story of the death of her young husband just as they prepared to enter a ministry together. She related the heaviness of her grief and the questions that emerged over why this terrible thing had occurred. She then told of the tremendous release that came when she could move beyond asking, *Why?* and instead ask, *Where to from here, Lord?*

What does her experience tell us about the meaning of Christian hope?

Questions:

1. Can you think of ways some have tried to deny the expression of grief by themselves or another in the face of some painful loss? Why do you feel we practice this denial?

2. Have you found particular comfort for yourself from some biblical truth about the meaning of death? Share those insights with others in your group or class.

3. In 1 Thessalonians 5:5 believers are described as "sons of light" and "sons of the day." What do these images bring to your mind about Christian living?

4. How does the example of Jesus' death and resurrection encourage his followers in the face of tragedies and threats?

Focal Text

2 Thessalonians
3:6–13

Background

2 Thessalonians
3:6–13

Main Idea

Daily work is a way of putting the
Christian faith into action.

Question to Explore

How does the Christian faith
relate to daily work?

LESSON
THIRTEEN

Faith That Works
in the Workplace

Study Aim

To identify ways Christians can relate their faith to their daily work

Study and Action Emphases

- Affirm the Bible as our authoritative guide for life and ministry
- Share the gospel with all people
- Develop a growing, vibrant faith

Quick Read

Christians must demonstrate their faith in the workplace, where much of life is spent, as a witness to their life commitment to Christ as Lord of all.

In the city where we live is a local grocery chain that consistently leads in market share in the retail grocery business of the area. These are not the cheapest stores, by any means. They do not bear a nationally recognized name. The stores do not open on Sundays, which most retailers see as one of their most profitable days. You can't buy beer or wine in these stores. So how do they consistently lead in market share?

The buildings are impressive, but there is more to their success than that. One need only observe the way the stores operate to see the difference. Employees are made to feel important in the operation of the store. Employees notice customers and go out of their way to be helpful. Ask directions to a product and you will likely find an employee going with you to point the way. An army of retirees as well as school-age teens is employed to bag and carry your groceries to your car. People often comment about the different "feel" of shopping in those stores.

Learning the history of the company reveals that the founder of the family-run business is a Christian who determined in the beginning to take his faith seriously in operating his business. His sons, who now make many of the decisions, follow in his faith footsteps and seek ways to put their religious convictions to work in the daily operation of the stores. They see their retail outlets as a way to serve the needs of people, and they seek to do business in a way that honors their Christian heritage.

Lesson 13: Faith That Works in the Workplace

Scripture holds a lofty view of the place of work in life. Paul and his companions noted a troubling trend, however, in the lives of some of the new Christians in Thessalonica. Either out of a misunderstanding of the timing of the return of Christ or a misguided abuse of the compassion and generosity of others, they had just stopped working.

2 Thessalonians 3:6–13

6In the name of the Lord Jesus Christ, we command you, brothers, to keep away from every brother who is idle and does not live according to the teaching you received from us. **7**For you yourselves know how you ought to follow our example. We were not idle when we were with you, **8**nor did we eat anyone's food without paying for it. On the contrary, we worked night and day, laboring and toiling so that we would not be a burden to any of you. **9**We did this, not because we do not have the right to such help, but in order to make ourselves a model for you to follow. **10**For even when we were with you, we gave you this rule: "If a man will not work, he shall not eat."

11We hear that some among you are idle. They are not busy; they are busybodies. **12**Such people we command and urge in the Lord Jesus Christ to settle down and earn the bread they eat. **13**And as for you, brothers, never tire of doing what is right.

The Undisciplined life (3:6)

The problem in a nutshell had to do with those described as "idle," as the NIV translates it. Unfortunately, this translation misses the depth of the Greek word. The New American Standard Bible properly translates it as "unruly" (3:6) and "undisciplined" (3:7). The issue is not simply that some had stopped working, choosing to live off the labor of others, but that they had adopted a meddling lifestyle that was out of control. Misplaced activity rather than inactivity was their real problem. First Thessalonians 4:11 had already addressed these whose work in life had become minding others' business. Perhaps the issue had worsened and warranted stronger treatment in this second letter.

> ... They seek to do business in a way that honors their Christian heritage.

The context of this passage needs to be seen in the light of the opening chapter of this second letter in which Paul addressed the congregation. "To this end we always pray for you, asking that our God will make you worthy of his call and will fulfill by his power every good resolve and work of faith, so that the name of our Lord Jesus may be glorified in you, and you in him, according to the grace of our God and the Lord Jesus Christ" (2 Thessalonians 1:11–12, NRSV).

Nothing was more important in the church in that pagan culture—or in any culture—than that

Jesus should be glorified. The lives of Christians should reflect the very best of the new creation that occurs through faith in Jesus as Lord. One way a human life can glorify the Lord is through the way one invests his or her labor.

It should be noted that the words of 1 Thessalonians 3:6 come as a "command" from the heart of the apostle. The same imperative tone is found in verses 10 and 12, indicating the seriousness with which these words were written.

Another issue that may be implied by this command has to do with the uncertain number of days any of us has on this earth. The Letter to the Ephesians later gave this exhortation: "Be careful then how you live, not as unwise people but as wise, making the most of the time, because the days are evil" (Ephesians 5:15–16, NRSV). We are stewards of life, including our work, which typically occupies the most of our waking hours. Stewardship has to do with managing our affairs out of a reverent and grateful heart. Life itself is a gift, and since work is such an important part of life, it must reflect a thankful stewardship. We must not waste life in useless or destructive behavior.

In advising the Thessalonians "to keep away from every brother who is idle" (2 Thess. 3:6), we should not read this instruction as calling for the expulsion of these people from the church. Paul still called such a person "brother," and in 3:15 the faithful were advised not to treat them as enemies. Instead they were to seek to bring them back to faithfulness. The church must be in the business of redemption, not seeking to exclude those who are not measuring up.

The Missionaries' Example (3:7–9)

The missionary team did not ask the new converts to do anything they had not themselves exemplified. Indeed, they used the example of their work as a way to demonstrate faith and the influence of the gospel on their lives. Paul and his team had sought to earn their own support when they came to Thessalonica. It had been one way they had demonstrated their sensitivity to those whom they brought to faith, and their desire not to be a burden on the new church. Although they might have considered themselves to have the right of support by the church, they would not accept it, choosing instead to earn their living by their own labor.

. . . Since work is such an important part of life, it must reflect a thankful stewardship.

It is interesting to see the various times in his epistles that Paul discussed his own practice of working to support himself. See 1 Corinthians 9:13–18; 2 Corinthians 11:7–9; 12:14; 1 Thessalonians 2:9; Philippians 4:10, 15–19. See also Acts 18:3, which describes Paul's work.

In 2 Thessalonians 3, work is described as a means of witness for Paul and his companions. The same would be true for the Thessalonian Christians if they would heed his exhortation. Taking faith to work is just one way of putting to work the truth Jesus shared in Matthew 5:16: "In the same way, let your light shine before others, so that they may see your good works and give glory to your Father in heaven" (NRSV).

Sometimes the settings where our faith is least expected to be expressed are the places where we can make the most impact when our faith is brought to light. Do your co-workers know of your faith? Can they see it in your work, your words, your relationships,

Scripture holds a lofty view of the place of work in life.

and your example? Paul could point to his example, knowing that his faith had shaped his work in their midst.

Some Special Issues Related to Work

For years I heard an interpretation of the Genesis account of Adam's sin that said that work was the curse put on him because of his disobedience (Genesis 3:17–19). Work, however, is not a curse; just ask the person who would so much like to engage in some meaningful labor, but who cannot.

We live in a time when many people have experienced the loss of jobs as corporations and businesses have downsized. Many of these people are learning a new respect for work as a blessing, not a curse. We need to have great sensitivity to what this experience can do to a person's sense of worth.

A great deal of attention has been brought in recent years to those whose physical disabilities limit or hinder their ability to work. Making workplaces accessible to such people has permitted many to experience the meaning of work in a new way as they contribute to their society. It is a thrilling testimony to the human spirit to see how much some contribute through their work in spite of what seem to others to be great disabilities.

In the warning of the text we are examining today, Paul is clearly not talking about those who would like nothing better than to be able to work and earn their livelihood. The issue here is those who are able-bodied, who could make a contribution to the good of society and yet choose to waste their days prying into others' affairs. The problem lies in their unwillingness or refusal to work.

> *. . . Our daily work needs to be a major way in which we put into action Christian love.*

From the beginning of creation, people were given a task. As the Genesis story tells us, man was placed in a garden setting and given the responsibility of tilling the soil and tending the garden (Gen. 2:8). Work was not a curse in response to sin but a blessing given by a benevolent Creator to give us a reason to get up in the morning! It would be through the labors of all of humankind, working with the resources provided by the Creator, that people would be fed, housed, and clothed.

A number of other New Testament passages speak of living one's faith in one's daily work as a means of accomplishing God's will for his people. For example, Ephesians 4:28 shows that one purpose of work is to have something to share with others in acts of benevolence. Further, Ephesians 6:5–8 describes an attitude toward work and workers by both slaves and masters, strange language in our culture but very appropriate in that day. Colossians 3:23–24 and Titus 2:9–10 speak of doing one's work with reverence and respect to the God of the universe, demonstrating honesty and integrity in one's work.

Work As a Labor of Love (5:13)

"Doing what is right" (NIV, NRSV) or "doing good" (NASB) was Paul's way of reminding his hearers about the importance of the day's work. The Christian's business is to live out the principle of God's kind of love (*agape*) in every aspect of life. It has to do with relationships with those close to us but also to the community around us. After all, "God so loved the *world* that he gave his one and only Son . . . " (John 3:16, italics for emphasis).

Perhaps the heart of the issue before us is to use our daily work a *labor of love.* To put it another way, our daily work needs to be a major way in which we put into action Christian love. Our daily work should be aimed at providing for others something that is helpful and needed. Our work should be consistent with our faith profession.

An oft-repeated story out of our nation's history has to do with the industry that provided parachutes during World War II. The process of producing these life-saving devices was largely a matter of manual labor. People were employed to work at their sewing machines for long hours, day after day. They cut and sewed miles of the same kind and color fabric, which was then packed and shipped to the bases that supplied air power for the war effort. Over and over the process was repeated with little break in the monotonous routine.

We are stewards of life, including our work, which typically occupies the most of our waking hours.

Someone asked how people could work like this without giving in to sheer boredom and mental fatigue. The answer was found in the schedule of each day when, at the beginning of a shift, the workers were reminded of the nature of their task. They were making life-saving devices, and they were challenged to think of how they would work at their task if they knew a son, a father, or a brother would wear that parachute.

Do you think they got the picture of the importance of their work? With that mindset it would be impossible to take their work with anything but utter seriousness. It became a labor of love!

That seems to be the same degree of seriousness which Paul and his companions felt about every Christian working with honor and dedication. The Thessalonian Christians might not be making life-saving devices, but the example they set in their daily labor might well be the means of encouraging or discouraging a wandering soul in an eternal decision with respect to Christ.

The nation pauses the first weekend in September each year to focus on the dignity of work and in honor of the men and women who labor to provide for our nation. Few things have the potential to bring to us more meaning, purpose, and fulfillment than our work. On the other hand, for many people their work is little more than an exhausting, frustrating struggle. How many people do you know who truly love their work? How many head off each day with a sense of purpose, glad for the privilege of having health and opportunity to work?

. . . We need to learn the biblical view of work as an act of worship, a stewardship of opportunities, and a means of ministering to others out of the abundance of God's resources.

Perhaps we need to learn the biblical view of work as an act of worship, a stewardship of opportunities, and a means of ministering to others out of the abundance of God's resources. At the very least, we need to see the opportunities in the workplace to do something constructive for the good of others, providing for our families, and bearing witness to our relationship to Christ through our attitudes and actions.[1]

Command

The word translated "command" in 2 Thessalonians 3:6 is from the military vocabulary of the first century. The word had to do with authority and power in those who were responsible for soldiers in battle. As such, the orders were to be taken seriously and without question. Obeying the commands might well mean the difference of victory or defeat.

The commander in a battle was a person who had earned the respect and admiration of his troops. The commander had shown concern for the soldiers who followed him. While the commander may have pushed these soldiers in training, he had demonstrated that it was all for their good. The commander might call for the soldiers to risk everything for victory, but such a call came from one who would be there with his people. Paul's "command" in verse 6 is presented as a command "in the name of our Lord Jesus Christ." Jesus has demonstrated beyond question his love of all who follow him.

Putting Faith to Work in the Workplace

In putting your faith to work in the workplace, consider these questions as you go about your daily labor:

- Have I really thought about my work as a gift through which I can honor God and give thanks for a job to do?

- Is what I am doing today merely in my self-interest?

- How is my work today providing for the true needs of others?

- Am I treating my co-workers with the kind of respect that reflects the love of Christ?

- Am I giving an honest day's work for my employer?

Questions

1. What are some of the ways we measure the value of a person's work?

2. Do you feel those measurements are valid? Explain your answers.

3. What qualities of Paul and his companions are worth following (see 2 Thessalonians 3:7)? How could we put them to work in our kind of world?

4. Do you feel that certain kinds of work are inappropriate for a Christian? Explain why you reach your conclusions.

5. What are some ways in which Christians can live their faith in the workplace?

NOTES

1. For practical insights on living one's faith in the workplace see this book: Ross West, *Go to Work and Take Your Faith Too!* (Macon, GA: Smyth and Helwys, 1997).

Our Next New Study

(Available for use beginning December 2003)

LETTERS OF JOHN AND PETER

1, 2, 3 JOHN: MEASURING AUTHENTIC CHRISTIANITY

Lesson 1	Really Living for the God Who Really Came	1 John 1:1—2:2
Lesson 2	Tests for Knowing God	1 John 2:3–11, 18–27
Lesson 3	Being God's Children	1 John 2:28—3:10
Lesson 4	Down-to-Earth Love	1 John 3:11–18, 23–24; 4:7–21
Lesson 5	Faith Is the Victory	1 John 5
Lesson 6	Be Wise, Be Generous	2 John 1–11; 3 John 1–8

1 PETER: FOR CHRISTIANS UNDER PRESSURE

Lesson 7	Keep Life in Perspective	1 Peter 1:1–12
Lesson 8	Focus Your Life	1 Peter 1:13—2:3
Lesson 9	Live Up to Who You Are	1 Peter 2:4–10
Lesson 10	Live Commendably in Your World	1 Peter 2:11—3:8

Additional Resources for Studying 1, 2, 3 John[1]

Glenn W. Barker. *1 John.* The Expositor's Bible Commentary. Volume 12. Grand Rapids: Zondervan Publishing House, 1981.

C. Clifton Black. "The First, Second, and Third Letters of John." *The New Interpreter's Bible.* Volume XII. Nashville: Abingdon Press, 1998.

Raymond E. Brown. *The Epistles of John.* The Anchor Bible. Volume 30. Garden City, New York: Doubleday & Company, Inc., 1982.

R. Alan Culpepper. *1 John, 2 John, 3 John.* Knox Preaching Guides. Atlanta: John Knox Press, 1985.

I. Howard Marshall. *The Epistles of John.* The New International Commentary on the New Testament. Grand Rapids, Michigan: William B. Eerdmans Publishing Company, 1978.

Edward A. McDowell. "1-2-3 John." *The Broadman Bible Commentary.* Volume 12. Nashville: Broadman Press, 1972.

Earl F. Palmer. *1, 2, 3 John, Revelation.* The Communicator's Commentary. Waco, Texas: Word Books, Publisher, 1982.

Stephen S. Smalley. *1, 2, 3 John.* Word Biblical Commentary. Volume 51. Waco, Texas: Word Books, Publisher, 1984.

D. Moody Smith. *First, Second, and Third John.* Interpretation: A Bible Commentary for Preaching and Teaching. Louisville: John Knox Press, 1991.

John R. W. Stott. *The Letters of John.* Revised edition. Tyndale New Testament Commentaries. Grand Rapids, Michigan: William B. Eerdmans Publishing Company, 1988.

Additional Resources for Studying 1 Peter

David L. Bartlett. "The First Letter of Peter." *The New Interpreter's Bible.* Volume XII. Nashville: Abingdon Press, 1998.

Ernest Best. *I Peter.* New Century Bible. London: Oliphants, 1971.

Peter H. Davids. *The First Epistle of Peter.* The New International Commentary on the New Testament. Grand Rapids, Michigan: William B. Eerdmans Publishing Company, 1990.

J. Ramsey Michaels. *1 Peter.* Word Biblical Commentary. Volume 49. Waco, Texas: Word Books, Publisher, 1988.

A.T. Robertson. *Word Pictures in the New Testament.* Volume VI. Nashville, Tennessee: Broadman Press, 1933.

Ray Summers. "1 Peter." *The Broadman Bible Commentary.* Volume 12. Nashville: Broadman Press, 1972.

NOTES

1. Listing a book does not imply full agreement by the writers or BAPTISTWAY PRESS® with all of its comments.

How to Order More Bible Study Materials

It's easy! Just fill in the following information. (Note: when the *Teaching Guide* is priced at $2.45, the *Teaching Guide* includes Bible comments for teachers.)

✦ = Texas specific

Title of item	Price	Quantity	Cost
This Issue:			
Philippians, Colossians, Thessalonians—Study Guide	$1.95	_____	_____
Philippians, Colossians, Thessalonians—Large Print Study Guide	$1.95	_____	_____
Philippians, Colossians, Thessalonians—Teaching Guide	$2.45	_____	_____
Previous Issues Available:			
God's Message in the Old Testament—Study Guide ✦	$1.95	_____	_____
God's Message in the Old Testament—Teaching Guide ✦	$1.95	_____	_____
Genesis 12—50: Family Matters—Study Guide	$1.95	_____	_____
Genesis 12—50: Family Matters—Large Print Study Guide	$1.95	_____	_____
Genesis 12—50: Family Matters—Teaching Guide	$2.45	_____	_____
Isaiah and Jeremiah—Study Guide	$1.95	_____	_____
Isaiah and Jeremiah—Large Print Study Guide	$1.95	_____	_____
Isaiah and Jeremiah—Teaching Guide	$2.45	_____	_____
Amos, Hosea, Micah—Study Guide	$1.95	_____	_____
Amos, Hosea, Micah—Large Print Study Guide	$1.95	_____	_____
Amos, Hosea, Micah—Teaching Guide	$2.45	_____	_____
Good News in the New Testament—Study Guide ✦	$1.95	_____	_____
Good News in the New Testament—Large Print Study Guide ✦	$1.95	_____	_____
Good News in the New Testament—Teaching Guide ✦	$2.45	_____	_____
Matthew: Jesus As the Fulfillment of God's Promises—Study Guide ✦	$1.95	_____	_____
Matthew: Jesus As the Fulfillment of God's Promises—Large Print Study Guide ✦	$1.95	_____	_____
Matthew: Jesus As the Fulfillment of God's Promises—Teaching Guide ✦	$2.45	_____	_____
Jesus in the Gospel of Mark—Study Guide	$1.95	_____	_____
Jesus in the Gospel of Mark—Large Print Study Guide	$1.95	_____	_____
Jesus in the Gospel of Mark—Teaching Guide	$2.45	_____	_____
Gospel of John—Study Guide	$1.95	_____	_____
Gospel of John—Large Print Study Guide	$1.95	_____	_____
Gospel of John—Teaching Guide	$2.45	_____	_____
Acts: Sharing God's Good News with Everyone—Study Guide ✦	$1.95	_____	_____
Acts: Sharing God's Good News with Everyone—Teaching Guide ✦	$1.95	_____	_____
Romans: Good News for a Troubled World—Study Guide ✦	$1.95	_____	_____
Romans: Good News for a Troubled World—Teaching Guide ✦	$1.95	_____	_____
1 Corinthians—Study Guide	$1.95	_____	_____
1 Corinthians—Large Print Study Guide	$1.95	_____	_____
1 Corinthians—Teaching Guide	$2.45	_____	_____
Galatians and Ephesians—Study Guide ✦	$1.95	_____	_____
Galatians and Ephesians—Large Print Study Guide ✦	$1.95	_____	_____
Galatians and Ephesians—Teaching Guide ✦	$2.45	_____	_____
Hebrews and James—Study Guide	$1.95	_____	_____
Hebrews and James—Large Print Study Guide	$1.95	_____	_____
Hebrews and James—Teaching Guide	$2.45	_____	_____
Coming for use beginning December 2003			
Letters of John and Peter—Study Guide	$1.95	_____	_____
Letters of John and Peter—Large Print Study Guide	$1.95	_____	_____
Letters of John and Peter—Teaching Guide	$2.45	_____	_____

Beliefs Important to Baptists

Who in the World Are Baptists, Anyway? (one lesson)	$ .45	_____	_____
Who in the World Are Baptists, Anyway?—Teacher's Edition	$ .55	_____	_____
Beliefs Important to Baptists: I (four lessons)	$1.35	_____	_____
Beliefs Important to Baptists: I—Teacher's Edition	$1.75	_____	_____
Beliefs Important to Baptists: II (four lessons)	$1.35	_____	_____
Beliefs Important to Baptists: II—Teacher's Edition	$1.75	_____	_____
Beliefs Important to Baptists: III (four lessons)	$1.35	_____	_____
Beliefs Important to Baptists: III—Teacher's Edition	$1.75	_____	_____
Beliefs Important to Baptists—Study Guide (one-volume edition; includes all lessons)	$2.35	_____	_____
Beliefs Important to Baptists—Teaching Guide (one-volume edition; includes all lessons)	$1.95	_____	_____

Subtotal _____

*Charges for standard shipping service:

Subtotal up to $20.00	$3.95
Subtotal $20.01—$50.00	$4.95
Subtotal $50.01—$100.00	10% of subtotal
Subtotal $100.01 and up	8% of subtotal

Please allow three weeks for standard delivery. For express shipping service: Call 1–866–249–1799 for information on additional charges.

Shipping* _____

TOTAL _____

Number of FREE copies of *Brief Basics for Texas Baptists* needed for leading adult Sunday School department periods

_____

Your name   Phone

Your church   Date Ordered

Mailing address

City   State   Zip code

MAIL this form with your check for the total amount to
BAPTISTWAY PRESS
Baptist General Convention of Texas
333 North Washington
Dallas, TX 75246-1798
(Make checks to "Baptist Executive Board.")

OR, **FAX** your order anytime to: 214-828-5187, and we will bill you.

OR, **CALL** your order toll-free: 1-866-249-1799 (8:30 a.m.-5:00 p.m., M-F), and we will bill you.

OR, **E-MAIL** your order to our internet e-mail address: baptistway@bgct.org, and we will bill you.

We look forward to receiving your order! Thank you!